The Amputee

MW01535076

By

John W Paffett

This book is dedicated to:

All those who are facing or have faced amputation recognising the journey they have all begun. It must also be acknowledged the many loved ones whose presence and continuous assistance makes such a significant difference in their lives. Thank you for the love, care, and devotion you consistently show which is often understated but deeply appreciated.

Acknowledgement

To all my fellow amputees, I acknowledge and celebrate your strength and resilience. Together we can inspire, uplift, and encourage one another to live life to its fullest, proving we can achieve greatness despite any limitations.

I would also like to thank Jim Clark for sharing his thoughts and experiences as a recent amputee who has shown such fortitude in his later years mixed with his indomitable sense of humour. Thanks Jim.

Table of Contents

The Ageing Amputee

Introduction

As an amputee for over half a century I have some first-hand experience of the impact this has, both good and bad. Passing three score and ten years the mind begins to focus on the influence this has physically had to date, and what is to come as the ageing process takes a firmer grip with the ravages of time showing.

As a young lad of sixteen I had a hemipelvectomy following five years of progressive pain, resulting in a cancer diagnosis. This meant to get rid of all the cancer, my whole right leg and part of my pelvis needed to be removed. It was physically devastating, but life is sweet when compared to the alternative of death. I have called it the Ying and Yang in my life, and I am grateful to have experienced life fully abled doing the things young boys do as they grow into adolescence before my amputation. On the Yang side it has been physically disabling but there are many positives I can recall, not just the empathy and understanding I have for my fellow human beings but the people I have met along life's journey to enrich me.

Having had little support and no counselling at all for my amputation all those years ago, my thoughts are now focussed on the latter end of my life as the ageing process takes its toll. I have explored many issues which have or will be affecting me in the future and wanted to share these for the many other amputees, or soon to be mature amputees, facing a whole raft of challenges.

We are all made differently both physically and mentally. An amputation can have a variety of outcomes both positive and negative, but it is useful to appreciate the many aspects one must deal with. There is not a lot of understanding in my view of these aspects in any great depth to the variety of needs required at times. With the usual rigours and financial restraints in place it is as well to be aware of what may lay ahead and what help we can give one another, including the support given by carers, family, and friends.

It is often underrated the role of others outside of the medical profession. If I see someone pushing a wheelchair, I empathise with the person being pushed, but I also admire the person doing the pushing. They are often the unsung heroes who help so much, sometimes unappreciated with an expectation of their services, often unpaid but undertaken out of love. As their role is essential to the well-being of the amputee, I have mentioned these people because without them life would be so challenging and unfulfilled, and they too have their needs and expectations to be considered as well. Many give us unconditional love, which is without conditions or limitations. They are our bedrock of support.

I have tried to cover the different types of amputation by way of how much is amputated and the reasoning behind it. Whether that be through war conflict, birth, trauma accident or like me, medical necessity. The focus on all of this is time, its impact by way of health, both physically and mentally, including the peripheral issues which help and support you.

I wanted to not just share my thoughts and experiences but have another's input to share their own personal experiences, chapter by chapter. Living in the UK we have the National Health Service unlike others where insurance is necessary but not always affordable. I made contact through social media with Jim Clark who lives in Phoenix, Arizona in the USA. Jim is quite a character who has embraced his new life as an amputee at an advanced age with his stoic determination sprinkled with humour, and his underlying willingness to help others.

James (Jim) Clark

Amputee Related Biography: -

I became a late, blooming amputee five years ago. My 'ampuversary' is April 23, 2018. I was seventy eight years old at the time and became a *Right Leg, Above the Knee Amputee on that day. I hate acronyms but I am called a RAKA.*

I am a type 2 Diabetic and prior to my amputation, I spent over a year in and out of hospitals, rehabilitation centres, on 24/7 intravenous antibiotics, Wound Care Clinics, Home Health Nurses, Bariatric Chamber treatments, to name a few, fighting below the knee infections. After a year as a punching bag, the doctors said, "We can continue treatment with no guarantee of getting things under control, or we can amputate." I said, "Go get the chainsaw and crowbar. I have had all the fun I can stand!"

Through all this journey, my family has been very supportive. My bride of sixty four years, my son, daughter, and four grandchildren have all stood by me. I am thankful for their support and encouragement.

Which brings us to this book. During my going through "Hell Year", it became apparent amputation was a very real possibility and I had some time to dig into everything I could find about becoming an amputee. I expect many of you had no time to prepare mentally, emotionally, physically, or intellectually. I am a very active member on several social media amputee groups, and the Amputee Coalition "A-C Connect" discussion group. I love sharing everything I have discovered with potential and current amputees. It is my pleasure to help John with his mission and hope in reading this everyone can take advantage of what this book provides.

Chapter 1:

Facing Amputation

It is always healthy to question such a decision as having an amputation. Unless it is through sudden trauma giving an inevitability to it because of the severity, then discussing the risks, benefits, and post-operative care is a good thing. This buy-in to the process is part of the initial journey and will help to clarify the persons understanding of what lies ahead. It should also enable the option of consulting a family member, or other, in helping the decision-making.

Fully informed consent requires the person to have a sufficient understanding of the proposed procedure, to agree to, or refuse the procedure. It is the consultant's responsibility to explain the nature of the intervention, its associated risks, benefits, and possible alternatives and to give a medical recommendation. It is the latter which will be discussed in more detail later.

The persons comprehension depends on multiple factors, including his literacy, the adequacy of the doctor or consultants' explanation including the patient's mental state and decision-making capacity at the time of the discussion. Some may be in a state of shock and not fully be aware of what is being said or even be in denial. If there is a serious injury, their comprehension may be compromised by pain, drugs, fear, and anxiety, creating a potential for selective hearing and unreliable decision-making.

If the understanding of any parts of the discussion of informed consent is in question, the consultant must take the time necessary to revisit any uncertainty to ensure there is a sound foundation for the decision. Informed consent discussions are often hasty and short, especially when time is of the essence. It is often appropriate to repeat the discussion with the person in a more methodical manner. If all the facts are presented and alternatives clearly discussed and understood, then the decision whether to amputate or not is clear.

It can often help to involve someone close to the person in considering the decision of whether to proceed with the operation. It should be someone considered to have a reliable capacity to help contribute to the decision making, trusted by both the patient and the doctor or consultant. A family member or friend is likely to have a better understanding of the patient's point of view and to provide support for sound decision-making. Encouraging the patient to consult with trusted family or others can strengthen, rather than diminish their self-determination. After all this, the final decision to proceed with the operation is theirs.

It is also necessary to understand the information and make a coherent decision with the doctor or consultant determining whether they have the capacity to decide. If they are deemed to be unable to decide, then a surrogate decision-maker is required. In ideal circumstances you have an advance directive that names a chosen surrogate, but this is not always the case. A surrogate decision- maker needs to be accessible and know the patient well. Often it is the spouse. The surrogate must be able to make the decision too.

If the person facing amputation has severe open injuries of limbs this presents major challenges in management. In bygone years the presence of a severe crush injury or a vascular injury was sufficient to warrant an amputation. However, the evolution of sophisticated microsurgical reconstruction techniques along with the development of modern skeletal fixation and reconstruction devices have made limb salvage technically possible even in the most extreme cases.

In the early days it became obvious that technical advances can be double-edged swords, and prolonged attempts at salvage may be a "triumph of technique over reason". In attempting the salvage of a limb, the question therefore is not "whether you can", but "whether you should or not." A limb which could be saved must never be amputated, is a good ethos for surgeons. Open injuries are common in developing countries, where most amputees do not have the access to modern prosthetic devices. There is then a need for objective and reliable methods of assessing a severely injured limb and for predicting a good outcome. The acceptance of amputation with the social stigma and psychological impact of amputation are quite different in various societies and geographical regions around the world. The cost and social support to help the person through the various reconstructive surgical procedures, and the rehabilitation process after amputation or salvage are totally different throughout the globe.

Many people in the less civilised locations are poorly informed about what surgery is involved and the likely outcomes together with the risks of complications. It can be very challenging to help people learn about the different surgical options and what is involved, particularly given the impact which pain medication and anxiety can have on a new learning process. Unfortunately there can be complications and re-amputation particularly in people with advanced arterial disease.

A shared decision-making consultation is deliberately designed to engage the individual about to have an amputation by providing accurate and unbiased information about all the treatment options. This allows people the time and space they need to deliberate on the path ahead given their circumstances, values, and preferences.

There is a lot of research being undertaken as to how surgical repair influences the cells that contribute to healing, which needs us to rethink how we repair blood vessels. If new techniques or strategies which are less traumatic to arteries are developed, or new drugs and compounds which promote specific cell generation, we may be able to influence healing and hence clinical outcomes. Amputation may not be the preferred option and could thus have major implications on how we ensure safer and more successful surgical procedures in the future. In the immediacy of trauma, amputation can be seen as fundamentally necessary, but with advancement and education there may well be the ability to protect individual's lifestyle rather than life change.

There are three types of amputation. Above knee removing part of the thigh, knee, shin, foot, and toes. In my case part of my pelvis was removed too. There is the more common below-knee amputation, removing the lower leg, foot, and toes. Then of course are fingers, hand, or arm amputation.

Amputation can be surgical because of numerous causes or traumatic, due to an accident or injury. The immediacy of a traumatic amputation obviously precludes the stages one faces when being told an amputation is necessary.

No matter what age, having to face amputation is a traumatic event. For myself I remember like it was yesterday, even though it is well over fifty years ago and being told, 'They want to amputate'. With this news, the thump I felt in my chest was almost like an electric shock, such was the impact to me personally.

We are thankfully all different and take such news in differing ways. There are stages many, not all, go through.

- **Denial**
  Having been told the dreadful news, some refuse to engage in discussion or ask simple questions about the planned procedure. Some do not accept the reality that their limb is missing, even post operative, which in part is down to phantom sensations. I can still feel all the moving parts of my leg, like the toes, ankle, and knee over fifty plus years later. If this denial continues it can lead to serious problems, which is almost a disconnection with reality and may lead to underlying psychological issues. If like me after a long period of illness, the acceptance is strangely a lot easier. This is because the potential outcome of death if the amputation is not carried out, far outweighs the certain death ahead. Sometimes in cases like this, the grieving process has already happened and does not need to be started again.

- **Anger**
  Depending on the reasons for amputation, the anger may be directed at the other driver if it was a car accident for instance. Often it is the medical team where this is directed, perhaps feelings of being tricked or cheated into agreeing to an amputation are felt. We are complex beings and sometimes our thought processes are not as straightforward as we think they are.

- **Bargaining**

There can be feelings of guilt especially with the 'sliding doors' effect. If only I had taken a different route, then the accident would not have happened. Did I knock myself or hurt myself when younger which caused the cancer to develop? Should I have taken better care of the small infection which started on my toe? The list is endless. There are also excuses put forward to delay the operation both short, and long term which is a form of denial.

- **Depression**
  Having been told the devastating news, it can for some, lead to a spiral of depression and a feeling of being totally overwhelmed by events causing an inability to process what is happening.

- **Acceptance**
  There are stages to this for everyone. Personally for me it was a day or two, but for many it can take longer because of individual circumstances. This stage may not be reached until later in the rehabilitation process. Once amputated there is no going back, only moving forward on a new journey.

One other aspect to consider is body image and the immediacy of this change. This is more associated with younger amputees which is likened to a sliding scale as ageing occurs. To some it is still important, whatever age, with the social and psychological reaction varying. The predominant experience in most cases is one of loss and it is not the obvious loss of the limb but also the resulting losses in function, self-image, career, and relationships which matter.

There is the other end of the scale with using coping mechanisms, such as using humour and making plans after amputation. I do believe the many groups available on social media can give both support and sound advice on all issues because the members are those who have gone through similar trauma and have experience to advise.

There is a need to understand the individual and their state of mind at the time. We are all different and none of us know how we will re-act to this type of awful news. In some, the refusal to accept any help offered is seen, as well as hostility. It can even manifest in becoming pre-occupied by the minutia to the detriment of any other enjoyment. One of the other forms this trauma can take is seen by demanding a high level of nursing care by clinging to the nursing care. The other form is psychological and social withdrawal, not wanting to see or engage with anyone. This may only last a short time and go away as adjustment to events happening are once again 'normalised' in a more acceptable way. If however this continues it may require psychiatric assessment in the case of psychosis.

Unless the cause is one of sudden trauma and needed emergency treatment, individuals will be fully assessed before surgery to decide the most suitable type of amputation and any factors affecting rehabilitation. This is an area of skill required by the surgeon because everyone wants the best outcome for the long term. I have often read about post-surgery operations required to alleviate nerve pain because the amputation was not successful in that consideration.

The assessment is likely to include a thorough medical examination to check the persons physical condition, such as your cardiovascular system (heart, blood, and blood vessels) including the respiratory system (lungs and airways). The assessment for those with other significant illnesses requires a more robust review to ensure the suitability of a positive outcome both physically and emotionally, or whether additional support is required. The doctor will also check the condition and function of the healthy limb to ensure the extra strain and work required can be accommodated. Other assessments will cover home, work, and social environments to see what help may be required.

It is quite normal to experience feelings of grief during this process and if a child is involved the family too needs emotional support. As an adult now I can only imagine what my parents had to go through with me, their child facing amputation or death. No support was given to them at all. The process will be distressing and overwhelming at times as there are the parent's challenges as well as the child's. It is important not to be dismissive of any feelings of grief because we all must work through our own feelings.

One thing which resonates still with me during my pre-amputation period when at sixteen I was quite ill with cancer was being visited by a girlfriend. She stayed at my bedside for nearly an hour, and we laughed and talked until she had to leave. I never saw her again, and my mother said she was so upset seeing me so poorly she thought she was traumatised by it. It is therefore important to be prepared for different scenarios both pre and post-operation as the impact on friends and family can vary significantly and leave lasting impressions.

When I was thirteen my grandfather had gangrene in his toes when he was eighty three. The lasting impression was the smell of his leg before amputation and his cries of pain post-amputation. These impressions should not be easily dismissed and preparation of visits and discussing what may lie ahead can be valuable to ease difficult situations.

It has been recorded that up to half of those facing amputation surgery welcome it because the suffering being experienced will be alleviated and a new phase in their life of adjustment can begin. There are also the practical problems for many, such as pain, learning to walk on a prosthesis, loss of income and in some instances the cost of ongoing treatment. There is also the concern about changes in appearance, the perception by others, which can be moreso for younger, more self-conscious amputees. Body image is another concern which may impact sexual intimacy and threaten relationships.

Whatever scenario unfolds when facing amputation we are all different and our coping mechanism may or may not be well developed or even thought through. It can be quite difficult to look any further than the amputation because of the major impact it will have on your life. Trying to understand this impact in the longer term is a big, black unknown which most have little experience of and is thus quite daunting.

Jim - From my perspective and experience as a senior ageing amputee, all my comments will be related to being an amputee in the United States and involved in a planned verses unplanned amputation. I had my right leg above knee amputation in 2018 aged seventy-eight due to Type 2 Diabetes related infections and complications with a total knee replacement surgery. Diabetes is the major cause of lower limb amputations with over 53% of all lower limb amputations diabetes related and this is increasing. My recommendation if you are diabetic or pre-diabetic is to do everything you can to keep it under control or slow it down. If you are over fifty years old, your odds increase exponentially! The projected number and percentage of adults with diagnosed diabetes will potentially increase from 22.3 million (9.1%) in 2014 to 39.7 million (13.9%) in 2030, and to 60.6 million (17.9%) in 2060. The number of people with diabetes aged sixty five years or older will also potentially increase from 9.2 million in 2014 to 21.0 million in 2030, and to 35.2 million In 2060. This is a concerning projection.

My situation was a progressive one-year declining situation, and I was one of the lucky ones. I had a year to think about the possibility and research everything I could find out about the surgery and life after amputation. My condition got to the point where it became a no-brainer to get it done.

Within a few days after surgery I found that everything, I thought I knew about being an amputee could be put in a thimble! My education had just begun. Not to be misunderstood because everything I learned pre-amputation was important and helpful. I just did not realise how much more knowledge would be needed to function at a reasonable level. I recommend learning as much as you can pre-amputation and be open-minded about learning even more post-amputation.

There are many sources available in the United States and I am sure similar sources are available in other countries. One major source is Support Groups. My suggestion would be to try and find one prior to surgery and attend a meeting and ask questions. The Amputee Coalition has over 400 groups in the U.S. as well as Peer Support Volunteers who will meet with you on a one-on-one basis.

There are also many social media Amputee Groups where amputees discuss and exchange information. Just enter the word, "Amputee" in the search field and a number will pop up.

Although you will not be able to be fitted for a prosthesis until you heal thoroughly, it is a good idea to talk to several 'Certified Prosthetists' to get an idea of how to proceed when the time is right.

Pain is part of the post amputation experience. Everyone experiences pain at different levels, and everyone is different. There is immediate post-surgery pain, but many people experience ongoing pain called 'Phantom Pain'. Phantom limb pain (PLP) refers to ongoing painful sensations that seem to be coming from the part of the limb which is no longer there. The limb is gone, but the pain is real. The onset of this pain most often occurs soon after surgery. There is a new surgical procedure called TMR (Targeted Muscle Reinnervation) Surgery. My recommendation would be to discuss this procedure with your surgeon prior to amputation and if they do not do it, find a surgeon who does. I believe it is important as I had it done and now have no phantom pain. For those who had surgery a while ago, it can be done post-amputation.

On final point and from a USA perspective, if you have reason to believe or even if you do not have reason to believe you may be a candidate for an amputation, do make sure you have a valid 'Medical Power of Attorney'. Remember too, if you ride a motorcycle your group has one of the highest rates of any unplanned amputation category and you cannot decide if you are unconscious.

Chapter 2:

A Positive Amputation

A positive amputation seems strange because of the physical disability it causes, but this must be considered when looking at alternatives. For myself, having had cancer for five years before it progressed to a life threatening culmination, it was certainly a positive amputation. A life or death decision. Given four to six months to live or losing the whole of your right leg did not cause me to anguish over the decision. Of course it was devastating to be told this but when you weigh up the alternative it was a no-brainer. It was killing me, and at sixteen life was sweet and death unknown.

There are open questions to explore when asking people what they think about their amputated limb? Do they consider anything good has emerged from their amputation. Nearly half of us consider that something good has happened because of the amputation and find positive aspects in it.

There are some open questions to consider:

How – How we lose a limb, or limbs can have a significant impact especially if it is by trauma. For instance war and conflict injuries, even road traffic accidents or the like can have long lasting effects. Many incidents result in post-traumatic stress, which if not treated may or may not last a lifetime with flashbacks giving rise to anxiety disorders. In these cases there is very little, if any, positiveness in the resultant amputation. If however it is congenital amputation, then this is normally positive.

Amputation resulting from a malignant disease is more long term because of the uncertainty of the operations success in ridding the body of it. As time progresses the optimism of success increases but it can, in the early years, be like waiting for the sword of Damocles to fall, such is the uncertainty. Initially every little ache and pain strikes a chord as to whether the disease has returned, but time is a great healer in this respect.

What – The cause of the amputation in some instances can be obvious but this is not always the case. For myself it was cancer, and the question was, 'What caused the cancer?' For the first few years it was constantly on my mind, and I revisited all the little accidents that you have as a child to try and remember how it could have been caused, but I never did find the answer. Perhaps the problem was genetics, and I was born with defective genes. These contain information to make proteins, and proteins control many important functions like cell growth. Genetic mutations can change how proteins function and may mutate changing proteins in ways which cause healthy cells to become cancerous. I guess I will never know the answer now, but I have wasted many fruitless hours thinking about it.

There are many cases of amputation around the world but record keeping in some locations are unreliable or non-existent. In the United States there are over one million, six hundred thousand amputations annually of which 10% of these are due to complication from sepsis. This is caused when people go into shock and develop small blood clots in their blood vessels, which prevent adequate blood flow to their extremities such as fingers, hands, arms, toes, feet, and legs. This is why close monitoring of post-operative amputees is necessary to ensure the wound is as clean and healthy as possible.

Where – This question has two points to discuss. One is where was the amputation done from a location perspective, and secondly where on your body was the amputation.

In the more advanced civilizations around the world the positive outcome of amputation is obviously higher than those less advanced. This focus is on the whole cycle of pre- and post-amputation. How they undertake the amputation to give future prosthetic wearing a better outcome is down to the surgeon's expertise. There is also the sterile location of surgery and post-surgery for the patient to consider.

In a pre- and post-operative scenario there can also be consideration to counselling needs of the patient particularly where patients may inwardly be struggling with the outcome of losing a limb or limbs.

Amputation on the body may result from trauma or spread of disease. It is then a surgical decision on every amputation as to how best to achieve the right outcome and give the best opportunity for future prosthetic wearing. In my case, having cancer, there was a need to ensure my body was rid of the cancer thus a higher extremity amputation was necessary.

When – If the patient has a disease, then often chemotherapy and radiotherapy are necessary to contain or hopefully cure the problem. I underwent radiotherapy for six weeks to stop the cancer cells spreading. Whilst undergoing this treatment the medical personnel were discussing my case to decide whether to operate on me or not. If it is trauma through an accident, the timing is normally immediate, which is often due to life-or-death circumstances at the time.

I remember years sixty years ago my grandfather showing me his toe, which had gone black with gangrene. This eventually culminated in having his leg amputated just below the knee, and all this at the age of eighty-three! I remember his pain and anguish from this, which never saved his life because the gangrene had spread. Maybe amputating earlier would have had a better outcome than those last painful months. Little did I know three years later I would be facing similar pain.

Why - Whatever the cause, the doctor's decision to amputate is made if the tissue destruction, infection, or disease affects a body part making it impossible to repair or endangers the person's life. Likewise, a trauma or disease that cuts off blood flow to a body part for an extended time can also cause tissue death requiring an amputation. In most cases timing is of the essence. I remember such a case when two amputees were getting their legs repaired at the Enablement Centre and one asked the other how he had lost his leg. His reply surprised me because he said he was on a 'bender' with drugs and went to a 'squat' where no-one else was and injected himself. He had been in a drug stupor for a couple of days, and when he came to, he realised one of his legs was over the other and the circulation had stopped judging by the changed colour of it. This had resulted in his amputation.

I have heard it said repeatedly when talking or counselling – Why me? This is often quite a normal overwhelmingly negative response. My way of countering this, which I did as soon as I knew I needed an amputation was – Why not me? I would not wish this on anyone else, and in my case, I was one in twenty-five million! Such were the odds of the rare cancer I had. Events like this just happen, it is life!

I have read, but not experienced, people being curious about their amputated limbs. This curiosity is another aspect of trying to understand, and perhaps find meaning in the relationship between the "physical self and psychological self". It is something I have not dwelt on though. My only thoughts are, I have one foot in the grave, or one whole leg in Heaven already!

We are all different, thank goodness, in our uniqueness as human beings and we thus approach an amputation individually. Having stated the obvious, we do mostly fall into categories of meaningful acceptance, which include some of the following generic statements.

- Mobility without using crutches.
- Increased activity.
- A more normalised life.
- Independence.
- Knowing who your true friends are.
- Have a working life.
- Improved health and well-being.

Emerson said: What lies before us and what lies behind us are small matters compared to what lies within us. This is such a profound statement which defines so much of the coping and acceptance process of amputees.

Jim - From a personal health standpoint, most amputations can be considered positive amputations. Statistically, over 54% of all amputations are caused by other medical issues like John's cancer, my diabetes, vascular issues, blood clots, surgical infections to name just a few. Most amputations remove where the problems reside and prevent them from spreading to other parts of our bodies where they create more problems and generally cut short our lives. From a purely medical perspective the problems have been taken care of. As a general indicator, trauma amputations are 45% and "Other" just 1%.

A person's age plays a major role in how we accept or reject the ongoing, future circumstances of a positive amputation or a traumatic, sudden, unplanned amputation for that matter. In my case it was a good thing. I was seventy-eight. I was moderately active but started having balance issues and fell frequently. The trade-off of a leg verses going in and out of hospitals, more surgeries and pain was a 'no brainer' for me. I thought, "I will just get one of them artificial legs and be able to get around well enough." Boy, was that a colossal surprise and an understatement!

A younger person will invariably view any amputation whether positive or traumatic differently than an older person might. There are however many older amputees who are highly active and their attitudes toward their amputation are different than mine.

My view on planned pre-surgery is once you determine amputation is a possibility, do your due diligence. The internet and its search tools are a wonderful thing if you have access to it. A doctor can recommend and suggest alternatives, but the final decision is yours. Learn as much as you can to ask questions and make informed decisions.

I have been on this planet for over eighty years as I write this and have concluded everything, we experience in our lives is related to our attitudes and decisions. It is not what happens to you in your life, but how you deal with it.

The brain is a marvellous organ. It lets us make decisions and determine what our attitudes are going to be based on those decisions. No matter how your amputation occurred, you decide how you are going to deal with it, no one else.

Chapter 3:

Medical Intervention

A medical intervention is usually undertaken to help treat or cure a condition and, in my case, the resultant intervention, an amputation, cured me of cancer. Medical intervention for amputees nowadays involves a comprehensive approach to manage the physical and emotional aspects of the amputation surgery. The goal of medical intervention is to provide long-term support and care to improve the quality of life of amputees.

Individuals who have had adequate warning and preparation in general fare better in the immediate post-surgical period, whereas those who do not receive such preparation tend to react negatively or with massive denial. Preparation needs to include a clear explanation of the reasons for the amputation and any viable alternatives. The exact surgical procedure required must be clear, and what the rehabilitative process needed is, following it, is essential. Anticipating and dealing with the various issues being faced, even if these are not raised themselves, can be of great help. Such issues as relationship with friends and family, degree of functional loss, work capability, costs of surgery and rehabilitation, sexual adjustment, and social impact. Some even worry about what happens to the limb, but I have always said I have one foot in Heaven already!

It is important the surgeon paints a realistic picture of the immediate and long-term goals for the patient and his family. By describing the amputation as a reconstructive method to an improved life is a much different matter than implying it is a mutilation or even a failure. Being positive, with a hopeful attitude will help. Giving a detailed explanation of all aspects of the surgery and the rehabilitative process with full response to all questions will help to diminish anxiety, anger, and despair.

In general, the greater the loss, the greater the difficulty in adjustment. There are, however, some instances of massive psychological reaction to small physical losses, such as the loss of a toe or a thumb yet minimal reaction to severe loss of several limbs. Above-elbow amputation brings with it great anxiety and frustration, and bilateral amputation is perhaps the most difficult situation of all.

There are both pre and post-amputation stages to consider:

Pre-amputation

Where there is ample time to be prepared for surgery, many welcome the amputation as a signal or start whereby the suffering will be relieved. With this acceptance may come degrees of anxiety or concern. I believe I was fortunate because I welcomed amputation and never experienced any anxiety or real concern. I just wanted it done and to kick-start my new life as I was only sixteen then and wanted to experience life.

Pre-amputation medical intervention is a necessary and critical step in the overall care of anyone who requires a surgical amputation. The medical interventions that occur prior to amputation are important for several reasons, including improving the persons overall health, reducing the risk of complications post-surgery, and preparing the patient physically and mentally for the amputation procedure.

The first step is a thorough evaluation of the persons medical history, including any previous surgeries, medical conditions, and medications. This evaluation is important because it helps the medical team identify any potential risks and helps make informed decisions about the best course of action. In older people the complication may be other serious or life threatening conditions which must be considered when formulating a plan.

Next, the medical team will perform a thorough physical examination of the affected limb, including imaging tests such as X-rays, CT scans, or MRI scans. This evaluation helps a medical team determine the extent of the damage and the best surgical approach to take.

Once the medical team has a complete understanding of the persons medical history and the extent of the damage to the affected limb, they will begin a comprehensive treatment plan. This plan may include a variety of pre-amputation interventions designed to improve the patient's overall health, reduce the risk of complications, and prepare the patient for the application procedure.

One important pre-amputation intervention is the management of pain. This management is essential because chronic pain can cause physical and psychological distress, making it challenging for patients to cope with. I remember myself how bad the paid was and the relief I found in taking liquid morphine. The amputation procedure and their recovery pain management techniques may include medication nerve blocks, or other interventions designed to reduce pain levels.

Another crucial pre-amputation intervention is wound care. The skin around the affected limb may be damaged, infected, or otherwise compromised which can increase the risk of complications post-surgery. The medical team then work to ensure the skin around the affected limb is as healthy as possible, prior to amputation, which may include wound dressings, antibiotics, or other treatments.

Treatment may also include physical therapy, which can help the person build strength and stamina, in preparation for the amputation procedure. Physical therapy can also help with post-surgery rehabilitation allowing recovery more quickly with a return to normal activities sooner.

Finally pre-amputation medical intervention may include psychological support. Amputation can be a challenging and emotionally difficult experience and the medical team may provide counselling, support groups, or other resources to help patients cope with the procedure and recovery process.

Post Amputation

Amputation is the surgical removal of all or part of a limb or extremity due to injury, infection, or disease. This procedure is often done as a last resort when all the treatment options have been exhausted. After an amputation, post-operative care and medical intervention are critical to ensure proper healing and rehabilitation.

Psychological reactions at this stage include concerns about safety, fear of complications, and pain. In some instances, loss of alertness and orientation is affected. Those who sustain the amputation after a period of preparation react more positively than those who sustain it after trauma or accident. Most individuals from a psychological point of view are, to a certain degree numbed by it, partly because of the anaesthesia and partly as a way of handling the trauma of loss. For those who have suffered considerable pain before the surgery, the amputation may bring much needed relief. For me a cancer pain changed to a healing pain, which I welcomed because I knew the pain would get less with time, not the opposite with cancer.

The first step in post-amputation medical intervention is wound care. The surgical incision must be kept clean and dry to prevent infection. The wound should be checked regularly for signs of infection, such as redness, swelling, warmth, or discharge. Antibiotics may be prescribed if an infection is present or suspected.

Pain management is another important aspect of post amputation care. Some level of pain will be experienced after the procedure, and there are several options for managing this discomfort. Immediately afterwards morphine may be administered to help pain alleviation. Pain medication, both over the counter and prescription, can be used to help reduce the pain. Nerve blocks, which involve injecting an anaesthetic around the nerves which transmit pain signals, can also be used to provide relief.

Physical therapy is a crucial component of post amputation medical intervention. A Physical Therapist can help the person learn how to use assistive devices such as crutches, or a wheelchair to move around. They can also help provide exercises to build strength and flexibility in the remaining limb. Later prosthetic limb training may also be provided to help the patient adjust to their new prosthetic and learn how to use it properly.

Psychological support is also important after amputation and the person may experience a range of emotions, including grief, anger, and frustration.

Counselling and support groups can help the patient process their feelings and adjust to their new reality. It is this acceptance, where you cannot turn the clock back to how things were, which can be hard to accept and is often a stumbling block in moving forward. This kind of intervention can be especially beneficial for those who were highly active before their amputation.

As the wound heals the person may undergo further surgical procedures to prepare for a prosthetic limb. A surgical revision may be performed to reduce scar tissue or reshape the stump for a better fit for the prosthetic, although this should be considered pre-amputation to avoid this situation. A bone graft may also be performed to increase the stability of the stump.

Rehabilitation starts immediately in the hospital and is an important phase which presents the greatest challenges to the person, the family, and the amputation team. Initially, the patient is concerned about safety, pain, and disfigurement, which may move to social reintegration and work adjustment. Some people experience and express various kinds of denial shown through bravado and competitiveness, which I have personally seen. A few resort to humour and their behaviour can be erratic. No-one knows how they will react until faced with this daunting prospect.

Once home and in familiar surroundings filled with memories, the full impact of the loss often becomes evident. Many new amputees experience a reoccurrence of sadness and grief with varying degrees of regressive behaviour. This may emerge as a reluctance to give up the sick role and a tendency to lean on others beyond what is justified by the disability. Some resent any pressure put upon them to resume normal functioning whereas others may go to the other extreme and reject any suggestion they might be disabled or require help in any way. An important point here is in showing excessive sympathy which generally gives the feeling of being pitied. What is of immense value in all these matters is the availability of a relative or a significant other who can provide support without damaging self-esteem. It can be a tight rope, with occasional spills, and for some be very demanding. It is the ripple effect of amputation and who it affects, like a death.

Wound care, pain management, physical therapy, psychological support, and further surgical intervention may all be necessary for the person to adjust to the new reality and regain their independence. With the right care and support many can still lead fulfilling lives after amputation. It is after all not a death sentence, only a redirection of your life. Life's new journey is about to unfold and embracing this is to accept it and all the different things ahead.

Jim – *This for me is the scariest chapter in the book! How are we supposed to know if the doctor doing our surgery is the right one for us? I live near Phoenix, Arizona in the USA and WebMD says it has 1,561 amputation doctors with an average of twenty three years of experience. Currently, 1,056 providers have noted they are accepting new patients. Only 221 of them, just 14%, have 5-star ratings! How do I find the best one out of the 221 for me?*

My story started with me going to the Emergency Room (ER) at a good hospital because my lower right leg was swollen and hot. A week earlier, I had fallen and landed hard on my artificial knee. The ER doctor thought an orthopaedic doctor should look at it. I guess they threw my name in a hat and one of them got my name. I had no initial control. Several days of in-patient tests and 24/7 antibiotic intravenous produced nothing. The doctor sent me home with antibiotics. A few days later, I went back in the ER. The ortho-doctor sent me to a vascular doctor who was uncertain. The fact that I am a type 2 diabetic was a major concern. I faintly remember someone saying they heard people with diabetes sometimes need amputations. It was the first time the "A" word entered the equation! I became very concerned at this point.

My leg by this time was like a basketball with fifty pounds of excess air in it. It was literally ready to explode! I begged the doctor to do something. He reluctantly agreed to try to drain it. An ortho-nurse said it was like a dam bursting, spraying a glob of stuff that looked like banana pudding all over the place! Knee replacement surgery was not possible until the infection was under control. Following this procedure, it was twelve very frustrating months in and out of hospitals, rehab centres, wound clinics, home health care, hyperbaric chambers, etc. Finally, the ortho-doctor thought the infection was under control and did the knee replacement. This was botched up by severing a tendon and he called in a plastic surgeon to fix it, who made it even worse. Infection then re-occurred. I started to search for different doctors and a lawyer.

I found a different 'Wound Clinic' with an excellent reputation. The head nurse took one look at my leg and said, "You need to see Doctor "X". Over the years, I have learned to trust nurses' opinions because they know the good doctors and the not so good ones. Doctor "X" turned out to be exactly the doctor I needed. He was an excellent doctor and a top 1% amputee surgeon. As it worked out, we jointly decided an above knee amputation was the only course of action. I felt confident in him and the decision. My mind was put to rest.

The surgery was a complete success! There was minimal post-op pain, no infection and the incision healed quickly. It looks like a beautiful belly button on the end of my residual limb!

Having an amputation is one of, if not the biggest life changing decision you will ever make. If you have the luxury of time to make the decision, do not waste a minute of your time. Do everything you can to learn as much as you can in the time which you have. Finding the right medical personnel for your personal situation is like casting a flyrod into a hurricane and hoping you will catch a trophy fish!

If this is your first amputation, then from my perspective you need to understand there are several stages of learning. The first stage is 'Unconscious Incompetence' which is stating, 'You don't know what you don't know'. You wake up from surgery and there you are. My good Doctor "X" prepped me about what would be involved in my post-op plan but until you experience it, it does not sink in. Basics like using a transfer board to get from the bed to a wheelchair or using a grab bar and one leg to get from the chair to the commode for the first time. You are now six months old measured in 'amputee years.' My new life had begun with a steep learning curve. I do not know why, but prior to amputation, I thought after amputation my life would pretty much get back to normal. It took a day or two in the rehabilitation hospital for me to realise, "That is not going to happen!"

I was in the rehabilitation hospital for fourteen days. I had physiotherapy and occupational therapy sessions twice a day, but other than that, I had plenty of time to think. Lots of questions were flowing in my mind like, "What about this? What about that?' How am I going to do this or that? I realize my attitude toward life may be different than most others. I am an optimist and a very positive thinker. My glass is always completely full, never just half full. Some people let amputation bury them, others grab a shovel and start digging themselves out. To me, one of the most interesting things about being a human being is we have the blessing or curse of making decisions. We decide how to handle what life throws at us.

It was time to go home and face another set of challenges. We had a two-story house with what seemed like Olympic hurdle size steps to the second floor! I slept in a reclining lift chair in my den for several months until I got my first prosthesis. After this I was able to jump those hurdles. My daughter is an occupational therapist, and our house now has every device known to man for an amputee either installed or available.

If you are having difficulty dealing with any aspect of your amputation, reach out and ask for help or go on a quest to find answers yourself. The only harm in asking for help is not asking for help. If you are in a deep dark hole, there are plenty of people who will throw you a lifeline.

Chapter 4:

Immediate Post-operative Recovery

I remember feeling immense relief after waking post-op and patting the bedsheet with my hand to make sure it was gone. I could of course still feel my leg as if it was there, but in checking for it, the relief sent waves of tension flying away which had been building up for several months. I really did not want my right leg anymore because the cancer in it was killing me. For me it was a good amputation.

I naively thought the pain was not too bad initially, but this was because I still had the effects of the anaesthetic in me. The very next day I had extreme pain, thankfully it was not a cancer pain, which had gone. I pressed the alarm button located above my head and within a minute two nurses were by my bedside. I explained the intense pain between deep breaths, and they quickly got me some liquid morphine. I was with other patients who at times needed this medication and they told me its nickname was 'jungle juice'. Within a few minutes the pain disappeared, which was marvellous. It initially made me drowsy, giving me a sense of contentment and well-being, almost euphoric. I just wanted to feel better in myself and for the pain to stop, and it did.

Over the next few days I did drink a few small glasses of 'jungle juice' as the intense pain slowly subsided. The Westminster Hospital in London was almost seventy miles away from my home and being only sixteen my mother stayed close by during my ten days there, before the transfer back to a local hospital near where I lived. Dad was only given one day off work to see me but came up at weekends. Mum saw me daily and I remember looking forward to their visits, but tired so quickly when they were with me. When looking back, the cancer had eaten away at my body, and I weighed only six and a half stone (41Kg), and my reserves were diminished.

I was fortunate because I never suffered from post-operative depression unlike some. I never thought about any decrease in self-esteem or any increased dependency it might give me. I just wanted to feel better and live my life. I know some amputees think a lot about their amputated limb, but my dark humour started early, thinking I now only had five toenails to cut, not ten!

I believe being quite young, my focus was not that of someone more mature. I know many with a positive outlook think about the newfound independence it will give them and experience a change in their whole attitude to life. Once they are mobile there will be financial benefits, perhaps working again. Maybe afterwards being relatively pain free has been character building in their life, much improving their coping abilities.

During this immediate post-operative stage, much depends on the reason for the amputation and the condition of the residual limb. I was fortunate insomuch as I did not have one, but for others it can be a focus. The psychological reaction covers many aspects and include concerns about safety, particularly the older you get. There is also the fear and complications of pain and general decline in awareness. My illness and time lapse deciding to amputate gave me some time to prepare, and others in similar scenarios react more positively than those who sustain it after an accident or through trauma. Often a lot of these negative thoughts are put on the back burner post op because of the anaesthesia but may slowly return with time. I remember being relatively pain free immediately afterwards, and it felt wonderful after months of physical suffering and anxiety. The cancer pain being replaced by a healing pain.

My in-hospital rehabilitation was ten days in London and a week in a local hospital where I lived. This was over fifty years ago and nowadays a shorter stay is preferred. This of course all depends on the circumstance around amputation and the individual concerned, which in some instance may require many months in hospital.

It is during this time when the medical team are closely monitoring the patients progress, but there is also their family to consider too. Pain keeps the mind focussed on what relief is available, but thoughts may move onto safety aspects and even disfigurement. Psychological issues surfacing need to me addressed to ensure the right support is to hand. As a rule of thumb, the greater the loss, the greater the difficulty in adjustment although there are extremes to small physical losses where the impact to losing a finger or toe is extreme. For others the acceptance of amputation comes easy. We are all different and none of knows what hidden reserves, if any, we must cope with events impacting our lives.

I remember three days after my amputation the physiotherapist visiting me, and after a brief chat she made me sit mid-way on the bed on one side. She walked around the other side of the bed opposite me and told me to put a sock on. Strange, I thought but did as I was told and immediately rolled into her arms. My balance and centre of gravity had changed dramatically, and I needed to re-adjust to this. At this time I was given a pair of under arm crutches to walk with, and my first few steps were so amazing. I felt as if I could fly, feeling so light without the whole of my right leg. It only lasted a day or two but what a marvellous feeling. She then gave me instruction on how to use stairs with crutches, and that was the sum-total of preparation I received.

There is no place like home, and I was elated to be home to be with the family and Mum's cooking. There was no comparison then between home and hospital food. Being in a busy hospital with the regime they have does not give much time on reflection whereas being home does. For some it is during this time the full impact of loss becomes apparent. Little things like using the bathroom or getting up and down stairs, even the pet dog jumping up at you and causing loss of balance brings it all home. Many are surprised at this realisation again because they thought they had already gone through it. This can be accompanied by sadness and grief or worse still a reluctance to move away from the 'sick role' they may have had for some time and being totally reliant on others.

The family unit is hugely important to give the right support at this time because too much sympathy can give rise that the patient is being pitied. It can be a fine line to walk at times as readjustment is sought without damaging self-esteem. A supportive partner who assumes a flexible approach, taking over functions when needed, or leaving it when the amputee can do it is a tremendous help. Beyond this is peer acceptance, which for young and adolescent amputees is deemed so important.

When single or widowed amputees get home, they may or may not have a family support network. Not everyone has this or perhaps wants it, but they may suffer more psychological distress whilst adapting to a new way of life. This is a consideration at assessment of the patient for their post operative transitioning.

If there are surgical complications, then this can lead to psychological trauma leading to despair and withdrawal. If infection or residual limb revision is required or even a poorly performed amputation this often leads to poor rehabilitation.

After coming home I remember the feeling of the first night's sleep in my own bed; you cannot beat it. There were still many questions to be answered but the really is no place like home. Nothing is impossible, and I remembered being told, 'Keep your face always toward the sunshine, and shadows will fall behind you.' My old life, with two legs, was gone forever and I have my new journey to begin. Little did I know then about the marvellous journey ahead of me.

Jim - Once I woke up from surgery and figured out where I was, I asked my wife to remove the sheet so I could see if it was really gone, and it was! I have always wondered what they do with the removed leg, but I keep forgetting to ask my doctor. It had a perfectly good, two-month-old artificial knee attached to it that my other surgeon botched up. My doctor declared the surgery to be 100 % successful. After about ten to twelve hours, the surgery pain suppressants started wearing off and the pain which replaced them was far less than what I expected. The next three days were normal hospital routine. Take the meds, change the bandages, blood draws for lab tests, stand with a walker, sit in a chair, and eat wonderful hospital food! The fact that my pain and discomfort were minimal and did not trigger any emotional or psychological stress was a blessing and much better than what I anticipated. Based on communication I have had with others there are people who have had a much tougher experience during their immediate post-op.

Three days after surgery the medical staff moved me by ambulance to a Rehabilitation Hospital. In the U.S., Rehabilitation Hospitals specialise in post-surgery recovery. They do not treat general illnesses and there are no operating facilities. I recommend you go to one of these if you have a major limb amputation as opposed to going directly home after surgery. Medicare requires that you have at least two, one-hour Physical Therapy (PT) or Occupational Therapy (OT) sessions a day to stay there. Unless you are gravely ill and do not do your workouts, the hospital will discharge you and send you home. Medicare will not pay if you do not participate.

The first major realisation I had was that I needed to learn how to adapt. I can no longer just jump out of bed to go to the bathroom or take a shower. Every move will need thinking about and planned before you do it. You are like a six month to a year-old child again. Even the simplest tasks and moves need to be relearned.

Another major realisation was inches, (or centimetres) matter. Now with limited mobility and balance issues, an inch- even a quarter of an inch - can make the difference from being able to do something or not do something. Strangely enough, I enjoy this part of being an amputee. I genuinely enjoy the creative exercise of figuring out how to be able to function at the best possible level. I get great satisfaction out of successfully accomplishing something, even the smallest thing.

For example, my most common, "Can't reach it" conundrums occur in the kitchen. I have been trying since I came home from surgery to get my wife to understand how important this issue is, but she struggles with it. We have a normal home with the cabinets set up for "normal" people. It is very difficult to reach things in the upper cabinets from my wheelchair because I do not usually use my prosthesis at home. My wife tends to push things toward the back of the cabinet, and I cannot reach them. If she left the cups, bowls, and glasses as close to the front of the shelf as possible I could reach them! It is just the difference of an inch or two. Same goes for the fridge. If she pushes my beer to the back of the fridge or at the back of the top shelf, even after sixty four years of marriage, it is grounds for divorce! Subconsciously, it may be her subtle attempt to curtail my consumption of golden brew, but it will not work.

Grabbers are my new best friend. I have eight or ten of them strategically placed all over the house. Strangely enough, I enjoy this part of being an amputee. I truly enjoy the creative exercise of figuring out how to be able to function at the best possible level. I get great satisfaction out of successfully accomplishing something, even the smallest thing.

The second day in the Rehabilitation Hospital a prosthetist my doctor referred to me showed up with a shrinker and a residual limb protector. I had an allergic reaction to the silicone in the shrinker and found the protector too cumbersome to wear. Both wound up on the shelf. This hospital had about twenty five to thirty PT's and OT's and an exceptionally large, well-equipped gym. The focus of my PT workouts was about developing my core strength and my arms and shoulder muscles. I did not realise how important this was going to be. Being so inactive for the year prior to my amputation, my muscles had atrophied significantly. I had to work twice as hard to try to rebuild my whole muscular structure. My recommendation if you know you are going to have an amputation is to do everything you can to build up your strength prior to surgery. Be sure to get PT training on how to fall and recover from a fall because you will fall.

My OT training went smoothly. My daughter is an OT, and I knew what to expect. I was able to breeze through it easily, but it is important to get instruction on how to do everything properly and get the equipment you need to function effectively. She made sure our home was secure and well equipped with every piece of OT aids known to man and after two weeks they cleared me to go home. I was grateful for what I learned but also discovered it was just the 'tip of the iceberg' and I was the Titanic. The next phase of life as an amputee was about to begin.

Chapter 5:

Prosthetic Usage and Considerations

For me, having worn a prosthetic leg for nearly sixty years it becomes an integral part of you and a necessity, if you want mobility, which in turn gives a degree of independence cherished by all. Some leg amputees prefer to use crutches and not a prosthesis, but we all have choices to make how we want to live our lives.

A prosthetic can never replace your lost limb, but you do want it, at the very least to be comfortable. I seem to have spent a lifetime trying to get some degree of comfort, but it is an unfulfilled quest which requires constant and regular compromise. It is like aiming for the moon and reaching the top of the telegraph pole, but you can only keep trying.

It is for this reason you need to have a good relationship with your prosthetist which requires a symbiotic approach where you can both feed off each other's problems and ideas to solve issues. In this way your goal, and the prosthetist are aligned. Selfishly you want this relationship to last forever because it is so important, but nothing in this world is constant and people come and go. Whether this be for other job opportunities, promotion, or retirement, it happens and will change the learning curve which again needs to be climbed.

In my view, one of the most important tools for an amputee, whether old or young is a prosthetic limb. These limbs are designed to help regain as much of the physical function as possible. They are custom made to fit the unique needs of each individual and can be made to replace a missing arm, leg or even part of the limb. Prosthetic limbs can help amputees stay active, maintain independence, and improve their overall quality of life.

The use of prosthetic limbs can vary on the individual specific needs, health, and abilities. Some may choose to use their prosthesis full time, like me, while others only use them for specific tasks such as walking longer distances or performing specific tasks. I remember when I was first given underarm crutches. Soon my upper body strength increased such that I was able to walk quite a distance using them, in fact I could walk much further with them than I could with my prosthesis. The decision to use a prosthetic limb is a personal one and should be made in conjunction with medical professionals and a prosthetist to ensure the best possible outcome. This consideration covers physical well-being, including strength and the emotional impact on the amputee.

There are several types of prosthetic limbs available each with its own unique benefit and limitations. The type of prosthetic chosen will depend on the specific needs and abilities. There is however another variable, and as in most walks of life, excuse the pun, it comes down to cost. As time passes the prosthetics have been developed in both material used and technology available. For myself over the last fifty years, my prosthetic was first made with aluminium which included many rivets. This lasted over twenty years until carbon fibre and more robust plastics were invented and being used. There were over the years some technological improvements in particular modularisation of parts which speeded up the repair process.

I have always likened the development of prosthetics to a pyramid. At the base of the pyramid are the below knee prosthetics, halfway up are the above knee and at the top are those to suit hip disarticulation and hemipelvectomy, like I have. I use this analogy to demonstrate the numbers involved. Thereby, the natural emphasis is placed in development and design to suit the needs of many, rather than the few. I cite this because not too much has changed for me, whereas the computer aided ankle and knee design to assist walking has been significant. I am of course pleased for anyone whose situation improves through technological or material advances.

I have noticed when any amputee from 'The Forces' arrives at the Enablement Centre for repair or fitting, the limb supplied is always state-of-the-art. This is where cost comes into the equation. The Forces budget, or account funding is separate from the National Health Service in the UK. Another significant difference is where insurance companies are involved, perhaps through a road traffic accident, or a court settlement. In this instance, where money is no issue, private prosthetic firms provide a bespoke service where state-of-the-art is the norm. With the number of visits over the years I have made for repairs, if it had been to a private prosthetics firm then the shareholders would be very happy. I do wish everyone who has had the additional bonus of design, comfort, and personal service, well because the spin-off will slowly cascade down to the many of us years later.

Lower limb prosthetics are designed to replace a missing leg or foot. Even having a toe amputated can significantly affect your balance. These prosthetics can range from a simple foot or ankle to a more complex one replacing the entire leg. Upper limb prosthetics are designed to replace arm or hand, and can range from simple hand, or wrist prosthetics to more complex ones which replace the entire arm. Hybrid prosthetics combine elements of lower and upper limb prosthetics which are designed to provide maximum function and mobility. Myoelectric prosthetics, which have motors and batteries, use electrodes to detect muscle movements and translate them into movement of the prosthetic limb. They can provide a high level of control and functionality. Passive prosthetics are designed to provide only cosmetic benefit and do not have functional capabilities. All this demonstrates quite a selection of different types of prosthetics to suit individual requirements, which again underlines the uniqueness of each of us and what best suits us or what best suits what we can manage.

Factors to consider when choosing a prosthetic are numerous but above all, comfort is the key criteria. I wear my prosthetic on average for sixteen hours a day every day, and comfort is paramount. Functionality is most important too, along with durability. My prosthetic, until recently, has never been very durable by way of noise. The creaks and noises emanating from my leg over the years have been a constant source of frustration, annoyance, and embarrassment which has been the cross I have been forced to carry.

The cost of a prosthetic if you must purchase one needs careful planning and consideration. It cannot be just a one off cost because of the ongoing maintenance costs required. I cannot stress the importance of individual physical change and how this impacts the prosthetic. Weight uniformity is important and the amputee's physical ability to fit and use it, needs consideration too. With the right prosthetic and support, the amputee can continue to live a fulfilling and independent life.

The one constant in all this is yourself. I find it is important to try as best you can to understand the dynamics of the prosthesis. If you can undertake the simpler adjustments or repairs, then it saves the trek to the centre undertaking the repair work. I have been fortunate, although not by chance, to live close to the current politically correct name of 'Enablement Centre' as they now call it. When I first started going there in 1967 it was called ALAC or the Artificial Limb and Appliance Centre and about fifteen years ago renamed the 'Disablement Centre' before the latest change to the 'Enablement Centre'. Such is progress and political correctness!

I know some folk travel many miles if they have moved house just to keep the same prosthetist because of the inherent knowledge they have between them. The small repairs I undertake are relatively simple and anything more than this would need an expert eye, especially if bolts require a specific torque value to be applied for instance.

My prosthesis to me has three elements to it. The socket, the knee to the socket and the foot to the knee. All three need to be aligned to suit my gait and walking style. Individually we each have our only little nuances when it comes to walking. No two amputations are the same. They can be close, but the variable is the person, which also covers height and weight. It is this alignment where the skill and knowledge of the prosthetist comes into the forefront. They understand what is needed and the dynamics at play. It is never just one adjustment but often numerous small tweaks to try and optimise the very best outcome for the patient. This adjustment can only be learnt over time and from hands-on experience. I have seen fresh faces arrive over the years with a marvellous understanding of the mechanical and physiology theory in which they have excelled in at university. It is then the practical hands-on experience where the interaction with the patient is very important and is a time based learning process interlaced with good people's skill. I believe it is quite a dedicated profession.

The alignment of my prosthesis does take some time to achieve. Firstly there is the alignment of my upper body where weight is shifted at every step. This is like seeing an imaginary line drawn through the line of force going through the centreline of the socket, then through to the knee and finally through to the foot. There is the angle of the foot going up and down to consider, and the left/right position required. The knee adjustment is crucial, and some time is spent on this. The positions are so numerous with these being, up, down, left, and right on each of the four corners of the knee joint. There is then the upper knee joint connecting to the socket which has a locking mechanism to unlock when needing to sit down. Each adjustment can have an effect somewhere else on the leg, and it is constant trial and error until you reach a compromise which is acceptable to you.

When I feel able to walk with some degree of confidence between the rails when repairs have been made, or I am in a 'fitting' stage for a new prosthetic, then final minor adjustment can be made. For me, when the leg swings through, there are only a few millimetres of clearance from the shoe with the floor. This is fine when you are on a flat surface, but roads and pavements have a slight incline. If you are on the wrong side of an inclined pavement, it can cause you to catch your foot as you follow through and potentially trip. I always look ahead and plan which side of the road is best to walk on to avoid this if I can. I will not even mention walking on cobbled streets or pavements which have nightmarish consequences for me.

Walking equals effort, and for many some degree of pain. As we are all gradually ageing, we have less effort and strength than our younger years. From an artificial leg perspective, the higher the amputation the more effort is required to walk. It is for this reason necessary to try and maintain your fitness for as long as you can, together with your upper body strength.

Apart from the first few weeks of gradually getting used to wearing a prosthetic, I do wear it all day. I was only seventeen years old when starting this journey, which has the advantages youth brings. On average I wear my prosthesis all day, every day, with the very rare occasion I do not because of severe pain or a wound. In a recent study the average time for above knee amputees reported 87.5% wore their prosthesis on average for thirteen and a half hours a day with 22% bilateral amputees (both legs) wearing them for 7.7 hours a day. This showed the significant additional impact of wearing multiple prosthesis. It is this continual wearing with ageing amputees which cause them to reconsider their usage because it appears to be too heavy, more uncomfortable, and painful.

I read a report recently where it was recommended for hemipelvectomies like myself to only where a prosthetic for no more than 8 hours per day. I wear mine for double that. This recommendation does not suit everyone. If I never wore my leg, then I would need some support to sit comfortably without it as the right cheek of my bottom is now not the same height as my left. I get back-ache after less than half an hour. Again this is perhaps the conflict between theory and practice.

In the older community, when faced with amputation, there can be a reluctance to use a prosthesis and with the greater age comes this greater reluctance. I have seen this happen many times during my own visits for repair. It is very challenging, requires motivation and good health both physically and mentally to cope with. In studies less than half of the elderly population achieved a household level of prosthetic mobility. In understanding the reasoning behind this you must consider other medical issues may influence this too.

Another consideration for a new or longer term amputee is the ease with which the prosthetic can be put on. Some dexterity is required and a strong grip to wear the prosthetic to enable belts to be pulled tight or sleeves to be put on. If there is a loss of this as age moves forward, then it complicates the ability to be independent, which most want.

The weight of the prosthesis is another matter because the higher the amputation, the weightier the prosthesis becomes. In my case the prosthesis weighs close to a stone (fourteen pounds, or nearly seven kilos) and is not easily manoeuvrable when compared to a few pounds for a below the knee leg. A little known fact is the whole leg weighs a seventh of your body weight, and an arm, like a head, a tenth. In recent advancements of materials like plastics and carbon fibre the prosthetics weight has been reduced a little. This lighter weight material will help decrease the amount of energy required to walk a little. With all of this comes consideration whether the amputee will still manage the increased exertion, blood pressure, heart, and breathing rate it takes to walk. When starting to learn to walk it is slow, small steps which are required, but as confidence and comfort improves, the faster walking will require more effort. The goal for all this though is freedom and independence.

One other aspect to the size, weight and length of the prosthesis is the effort required to dress. It is one aspect for me that I dislike, having known before my amputation how easy it was to get dressed. I need a bed for instance to lay my prosthesis on to change my socks, put trousers on, then a shoe. Even when I must try another leg on when having a repair it is difficult because only having a chair next to you tests your dexterity. Even putting a shoe on with the ravages of arthritis is testing.

For a new amputee the prosthetic training will help enormously with a clear focus on balance, stability, and stance. Also depending on the type of amputation, for above knee (AK) there can be stability coming from a locked knee. It takes time to be confident to know and be reassured the leg you are wearing and walking on is 100% safe and will not let you down. It can knock you back if you have a fall. For myself I usually have two or three falls a year. I tried a locked knee when walking over rough terrain, but it was a noisy locking mechanism. When I came to sit down, not only did I have a knee lock, but I also had a hip lock. It seemed such a rigmarole to have to unlock both to sit down and I never used the knee lock again. It really is an individual choice of what suits you and what you are most comfortable doing in a safe manor. With some it helps to have a walking aid or a stick, and some training is necessary because the tendency is to lean over rather than stand upright, and bad habits are formed.

With technology nowadays changing rapidly, the advancements in prosthetic technology have become an area of intense research and development. All the different types of prosthetics can be either dynamic or passive. Passive prosthetics are basic, nonmechanical devices which provide support and stability, whereas dynamic prosthetics use advanced mechanical components to mimic the movement of a natural leg. Upper limb prosthetics are designed for amputees who have lost an arm, or a hand. These prosthetics can range from basic hook style devices to advanced robotics. They can replicate the movement of fingers and wrists, partial hand, and foot prosthetics which are designed for amputees who have last digits or parts of their feet.

Recent advancements in prosthetics technology have focused on improving the functionality and comfort of prosthetics. Some notable innovations in technology include neuro muscular control. This innovation uses microprocessors to interpret signals from the user's residual limb and translate them into movement in the prosthetic limb. This technology allows amputees to control the prosthetic limb intuitively and enables more natural movement.

There is a new procedure called osseointegration which involves implanting a titanium rod into the bone, which then connects directly to the prosthetic limb. This technology provides a stronger and more stable connection between the prosthetic limb and the user's body. This method has become popular with lower limb amputees who want a more stable and comfortable prosthetic. The result of this is much improved walking capability but there are some downsides too. Sometimes there is failure of this procedure because of the medical background of the amputee. This can include if they smoke, their bone quality, bone grafting, irradiation, bacterial contamination, and preparatory lack of preoperative antibiotics along with the degree of surgical trauma. Signs of rejection may include increased pain at the implant site, swelling, fever, and chills. For some it has been almost life changing but is not suitable for everyone. Talking to a friend recently he said he would not even consider doing it because he had already lost his leg through sepsis and would always be concerned with this repeating itself.

I have recently seen a middle aged woman with an HD (Hip Disarticulation) who has had an osseointegration and the results in comfort, walking style and ability was tremendous. I do feel this is the way of the future for some people with high amputations, especially the younger ones.

Another innovation is mind-controlled prosthetics using brain computer interfaces to allow amputees to control their prosthetics using their thoughts. It sounds almost like technology out of Star Wars, but excitingly it is happening now. It is though, early days and the technology is still in the experimental stage but truly there is great potential for it.

Amputee prosthetic innovation has come a long way in recent years. The incorporation of neuromuscular control systems, 3D printing, osseointegration and mind controlled prosthetics has revolutionised the prosthetics industries. They have also improved functionality, comfort, and aesthetics of the prosthetics providing amputees with greater mobility, independence, and quality of life. Further research and development will undoubtedly bring even more exciting innovations to the amputee prosthetic field. Initially a lot of this innovation is costly, and few can afford it, but with success, comes a higher order book which brings costs down.

While prosthetic technology has come a long way, the ultimate solution for amputees would be to regenerate their lost limbs. While this may seem like science fiction there have been significant advancements in limb regeneration in animals and some researchers are optimistic about the possibility of limb regeneration in humans.

Limb regeneration is a process that occurs naturally in some animals, such as salamanders, and starfish. These animals can regenerate limbs fully, including nerves, muscles, and bones. The process involves the activation of specific cells that form a blastema, which is a lump of undifferentiated cells that can differentiate into various cell types. This can then form the missing organ. Research into limb regeneration is still in its early stages but there have been promising developments in the field.

One breakthrough in limb regeneration research occurred in 2017 when scientists at the Keck school of medicine, at the University of Southern California, were able to regenerate a functional limb in a mouse using stem cells. The researchers used a combination of biological and chemical signals to stimulate the cells to form a blastema which then grew into a fully functional limb. They have also managed to regrow a tail for a gecko and other lizards.

The possibility of regaining function through natural regeneration remains out of reach for us amputees although it would be mind-blowing if this would happen in my lifetime. Scientists at the Wyss Institute at Harvard University and Tufts University have brought some success to the goal of regenerative medicine. On adult frogs, which are naturally unable to regenerate limbs, the researchers were able to trigger regrowth of a lost leg. It did take eighteen months to regrow a functional leg, therefore the broad parameters are in sight. Just thinking about a whole leg, like me, when compared to a frog's legs taking eighteen months, it could take a lifetime to grow! Thwarted again!

Many creatures already have the capability of full regeneration of at least some limbs, including salamanders, starfish, crabs, and lizards. We humans are capable of closing wounds with new tissue growth, and our livers have a remarkable, capability of regenerating to full size after a 50% loss, but not limbs.

There is a huge market for limb regeneration in humans to be a worthwhile investment, but doctors are still unable to induce human limb regeneration. It will happen, but in the medium-term future, as knowledge of regeneration and stem cell technology improves, including new innovative discoveries still to happen. It will be such an exciting time and I wish I could be around to experience this.

Another promising area of research is the use of gene editing to activate genes necessary for limb regeneration. Researchers have identified several genes involved in the regeneration process and have used gene editing technology to activate these genes in animals. While this approach is still in the experimental stages it shows great potential for future limb regeneration in humans.

There are still significant challenges to overcome, and one significant challenge is the complexity of the human body. Human limbs are more complex than those of animals which can regenerate limbs, and replicating the intricate structures of limbs in humans would be a significant challenge. Another challenge is the immune response. When the limb is lost the immune system recognises the injury as a foreign object and begins to attack it. This immune response can make it difficult for the body to regenerate the limb fully.

There are also the ethical implications of limb regeneration which should be considered. If a limb regeneration is possible, it could raise questions about when it is appropriate to use this technology and who should have access to it thus ensuring it is used safely and responsibly. I do still ponder how long it would take to grow a whole right leg for me!

Jim - Prior to realizing you are about to have an amputation most people have no idea what defines a good prosthetic. We just call them 'artificial whatever's' – legs, arms, hands, etc. If most new amputees are like I was, they may think, 'I will have my amputation, get an artificial leg and be on my way'. Nothing could be further from the truth and the reality of each person's individual experience. It is the most complex phase of the entire process of becoming an amputee. For example, one of the first decisions is which prosthetist will I work with? Currently, there are approximately 3,500 Certified Prosthetists, (CP's), in the United States. Most of them are in the larger metro areas. An amputee living in a rural location will have a limited number, if any, available. With 3,500 CP's, no two are alike in personality, skill and experience levels, equipment biases and ability to have a good rapport with each patient. The old saying, "You have got to kiss a lot of frogs in order to find a Prince" applies to this process. In five years, I have worked with four different offices and six different CP's, and I am still kissing frogs. I have good relationships with all of them but due to several fit factors, I have not been able to get a good fitting socket but keep trying. Getting a proper fit can be a long and involved process. I recommend doing everything you can to find a CP you trust and feel comfortable working with.

Then there is the equipment! There are hundreds if not thousands of companies world-wide manufacturing many more thousands of pieces of equipment for the prosthetic market. The global market for artificial limbs is estimated at US $2.3 Billion in the year 2022 and is projected to reach a revised size of US $3.2 Billion by 2030. Which ones are best for your individual situation and needs? Here again, you are relying on your prosthetist to look out for your best interests. They all have their favourite suppliers and biases. I have gone through numerous sockets and knees, ankles and feet looking for the best fit for me and suspect this will be ongoing for the rest of my life. While you will rely heavily on your prosthetist, do not be reluctant to stand your ground and if need be, change prosthetists.

New technology in equipment has really advanced in recent years. One major innovation, while being used longer in Europe and other parts of the world is now accelerating in the U.S. since being approved by our FDA is osseointegration. This is an advanced reconstructive surgery technique for amputees which eliminates the need for a traditional prosthesis. The implant connects directly with the bone of the residual limb and osseointegration patients regain body awareness which improves their balance and gait. While complications can occur, many people who have had it done after unsuccessful attempts to use traditional sockets swear by it.

Getting a proper fitting and reliable prosthetic requires another element which is, who is going to pay for it? In the United States, this is a major problem for many people. Medicare is the 'Bell Cow' for the medical insurance industry. They pay 80% of the expenses only when they agree with the necessity. It is a laborious time consuming process to get approval and many times payment is not approved. Same holds true for private insurance companies who follow the Medicare guidelines. I also have a very expensive 'Supplemental Coverage Plan' that picks up the 20% not covered by Medicare. It is a serious expense for me, but it has been beneficial by covering not only my amputee related expenses but also my other types of medical costs.

There are social media groups working to get insurance fairness for amputees. One very active group is the Amputee Coalition which in addition to advocating for change at the national, state, and local level also provide help and information for all amputees.

The last five years of fighting to get a proper fitting prosthesis which I felt confident with to try and be more mobile has been a struggle. Now in my eighties, I have concluded for me to be able to reasonably function I would consider converting over to an electric wheelchair for use outside my home *and a wheelchair accessible van if my current socket is not a good fit. If I was in the twenty to sixty age brackets, I would still be fighting but at my age, the path of least resistance looks appealing.*

Chapter 6:

Pain and Its Management

I had never in my life experienced the initial pain I had from the cancer in my leg. It was quite bad and over the next five years it got progressively worse. It was not a constant pain, more a shooting pain lasting a few intense seconds, every time emanating from my lymph glands in my right groin. Post-operation was more manageable because with the ring of a bell by my hospital bedside, a nurse would appear, and I would ask for pain relief. That was planned and expected relief, but worse is unplanned and unexpected pain, without relief.

Just after my amputation I experienced two episodes of pain, which have been the worst in my whole life. I still vividly remember it even though it was over fifty years ago. Some things are indelibly etched in your mind for life. My operation was a hemipelvectomy. This involved removing my whole right leg and part of my pelvis. The cheek of my bottom was then pulled around and stitched together, from my crotch to my remaining part of my hip bone. There were twenty six stitches in all and as amputations go, it looked quite neat.

It was nearly two weeks before the stitches needed to be removed and as I had previously had a biopsy a year prior to this, leaving a six inch scar, I was not perturbed by their removal. It was uncomfortable then but nothing too painful. The scar line along the amputation had been weeping quite badly and scabbing had formed along the whole line about ten inches (250mm) long. The difference this time when compared to the biopsy was it seemed all the nerve endings along this scar line were exposed or just below the surface. The nurses prepared me for the removal of the stitches, and I did not think too much about what lay ahead. I just assumed it would be uncomfortable again. How wrong was I!

To remove each of the twenty six stitches, the scab over each one had to be lifted or removed. I am unsure what had happened during the amputation to cause such strange hyper-sensitivity around this area, but it was sheer agony for every single stitch being removed. If I had known the pain involved, I would have asked to be given a local or even general anaesthetic. It was excruciating pain I experienced, and it lasted about twenty minutes until all the stitches had been removed. Even to this day the hyper-sensitivity still exists, and I cannot bear anyone touching it. This was real and awful nerve pain which hurt me.

My second experience of real pain was handed to me a few days later. I had been lying in bed a long time, even before my amputation, and this had caused a bedsore. It was rather painful, and the concern unbeknown to me, was the cancer had returned. It was just above my coccyx. When I was examined, it was found to be a double headed carbuncle in the middle of a bedsore. No wonder it was so painful, and the decision was made to extricate the carbuncle. Bed sores are painful on their own but add to that a double headed carbuncle and you have some serious pain to go through to remove it. Again if I had known the pain involved, I would have asked for some anaesthetic, but none was given, unfortunately. The pain involved seemed to match the removal of the stitches and the two nurses involved spent ages ensuring the deep seated roots of each carbuncle was removed. I have been fortunate to have never experienced any similar prolonged pain from each experience since.

This was part of my pain experience, but it is somewhat unique to what each one of us may experience. We all have different pain thresholds, and one person's experience is difficult to compare with another. Intense pain can be difficult to describe. The medical profession is agreed however that nerve pain is the worse pain to get. It was also a strange thing to do but I did embrace the 'healing' pain I was getting as opposed to the cancer pain because I knew it was lessening not increasing every day.

When you look at pain management there are stages for this. There is for many, like me, existing pain normally from a pre-existing medical condition and some form of medication may have already been prescribed. Once amputation has been undertaken there are stages of medication given to be effective in pain management on a reducing scale.

Firstly there is the anaesthetic which after a day or two wears off and the next stage follows, which for me was the opioid, liquid morphine. Sometimes this is administered to a patient in a controlled way as a peripheral nerve catheter. Stages after this for example may include ketamine as a receptor blocker, tramadol, or gabapentin, although the latter two never effectively worked for me in reducing phantom pain. Slowly after surgery there is a transition from acute pain to chronic pain. In the same way whatever medication is being taken should be reduced accordingly to avoid dependence.

Pain medication dependency is a serious concern after amputation, as the use of these medications can lead to addiction and other health complications. Individuals who take opioids for extended periods of time may develop a tolerance, meaning they need higher doses to achieve the same level of pain relief. It is this which can lead to dependence, where the individual experiences withdrawal symptoms if they stop taking the medication abruptly.

To avoid this dependency healthcare professionals must carefully monitor the usage and work with the person to develop a pain management plan. This plan may include the use of non-opioid pain medications, or non-steroidal anti-inflammatory drugs, which can be effective in managing mild to moderate pain.

In addition to medication there are non-pharmacological pain management strategies that can help individuals manage their pain such as physical therapy, acupuncture, and relaxation techniques. These methods can be used alone or in combination with medication to provide more comprehensive pain relief.

It is also essential that individuals who are prescribed opioids after amputation are aware of the potential for dependency and understand how to use the medication safely. They should take the medication only as prescribed and under the supervision of a healthcare professional. There is a need to regularly evaluate someone's pain management plan to ensure it is effective and safe. If an individual is showing signs of dependency or addiction, healthcare professionals may recommend tapering off the medication or transitioning to a different pain management strategy. By taking these steps individuals can manage their pain effectively while minimising the risk of addiction or other health complications.

From my own personal experience the advice I was given fifty plus years ago was to take some strong pain killers for mild to moderate pain, at the time these were called Distalgesic. I was told to take two every four hours, four time a day and they expected this would be for the rest of my life. I soon stopped these as the pain eased, and only took them when bad pain re-occurred. Sometimes you must listen to your body. If I had no pain, why take pain killers!

I believe we all must find what best suits us and nowadays there is a focus on CBD (cannabidiol) which is a natural substance present in the hemp plants and bred for nutritional purposes. The CBD is primarily extracted from hemp paste, made from the leaves and flowers of the hemp plant. I recently went on a University survey about the effectiveness and use of CBD. I only tried this twice whilst having considerable phantom pains and it made no recognizable difference, but maybe I should have persevered for better results. What works for me about 70% of the time is taking a couple of paracetamols and a non-steroidal anti-inflammatory drug like ibuprofen.

In some older amputees where there is everyday confusion then careful control of medication administered needs to be a priority. The health of each person and any underlying health issues causing reaction to medication given needs medical advice. Such side effects like a dry mouth, diarrhoea, reduced appetite, drowsiness even fatigue are all indicators of symptoms to be monitored.

During this immediate post-operative stage, support will be required for any residual stump wrapping which will include elevating the surgical site. There are other numerous things which may or may not help such as massage and cold therapy for muscle spasm relief.

There is another approach worth mentioning here and that is the Transcutaneous Electrical Nerve Stimulation (TENS) machine, although if you have a pacemaker or another electrical or metal implant in your body then this is not for you. Even if you are pre-disposed to epilepsy then this is a no-no. The battery-powered portable machine generates electrical currents, which are delivered through the skin via electrodes attached to the skin surface. What it does is to accelerate functional and motor recovery, and when used causes muscular twitches, leading to muscle stimulation. This activation of underlying nerves can in some, not all, cases give pain relief. It did not work for me, but everyone is different.

When looking at social media sites about amputees there is much dialogue about pain control and a whole array of differing views on what works. The one thing which sometimes works for me if I have bad pain in the middle of the night is to get up, have a hot shower and then put my prosthesis on. It often alleviates the pain somewhat and may result from different pressure points being applied to the area of the body giving pain. It really is trial and error, and after all these years I still do not have all the answers and will willingly try something new if it comes on the market because sustained pain over a long period is very debilitating.

Pain in amputees is not necessarily associated with the residual limb as other body dynamics come into play. There are the obvious stresses over time for those having a long-term amputation. The daily stresses and strains of everyday life on the limb(s) may have a detrimental effect such as scoliosis, arthritis, or osteoporosis. For instance hopping around on one leg over time can compound issues with knee joints. This can lead to disabling and progressive problems, and some are even seen as causing the same difficulty as phantom pains, such is the debilitating effect.

No-one wants to hear about pain issues day in and day out, and there is in the older generation, and particularly war veterans, the 'stiff upper lip' approach of suffering in silence. This can lead to issues of depression if not recognised or dealt with. Some make little use of problem solving or getting emotional support even giving up on medical assistance. This can lead to alternative downward spirals in drink or substance abuse.

When the time is medically and emotionally right after the amputation, a prosthesis can be made to suit the individual. Most want this process done as quickly as possible to get some degree of normality back into their lives, but it is a process not to rush. After the trauma of surgery the residual limb will take several months to heal including the swelling to reduce. This often leads to frustration and anxiety particularly if complications arise or the healing is prolonged. This is different in each case because of other underlying health issues or surgery complications. Whatever the issue, if the leg is measured for a prosthesis too early then the socket will only be comfortable for a short period of time until the body shape changes. It really is important to wait until the swelling has goes down and the scarring is fully healed.

Once the time is right from a physical sense then the bespoke limb can be made. This is when a period of pain must be gone through but is nothing like phantom pains. In fact you could call it some discomfort rather than pain. Your skin needs to harden and pressure points found and established to support the prosthesis. It takes both time and perseverance, but the rewards are well worth it.

Once a good fitting leg is made, practice in walking is the order of the day until the body is sufficiently hardened to cope with the new rigour and balance it must adopt. It is then necessary to understand your limitations. What speed are you comfortable in walking, and how far can you manage to walk before starting to feel the exhaustion? Balance is important and a frame, crutches or walking stick may help to begin with or even use longer term. It is understanding this and the residual impact it leaves on you. If one day you walk several miles, then there may be sores or cuts happening on your residual leg. In my case, if I walk several hundred yards then I suffer immensely for many days afterwards. Even temperature affects me, and I find it far more difficult walking in hot weather. It is simply understanding what you can and cannot do and the consequences of pushing the boundaries. These boundaries take a long time to fully appreciate the limitations or consequences.

The one good thing about pain experienced from your prosthesis is it is less severe than phantom pains. The only caveat I make from personal experience is to try and be aware of damage being caused around the amputation scar line. There is an area up to an inch (25mm) either side of the scar for me where there is no, or only partial feeling experienced. If your pressure point is along or crosses a scar, and you cannot feel any damage being caused then it can be a long time healing afterward. The skin here is taut and takes longer to heal and may mean having to not wear a prosthesis for several days until healing is complete. Fortunately a couple of paracetamols would be sufficient normally to offset the pain unless like me it can sometimes trigger phantom pains.

One other therapy effectively use is cognitive-behavioural therapy including relaxation techniques and biofeedback. Using these methods can help amputees learn to manage pain effectively and improve their quality of life.

With the prosthesis you get pain and this needs to be considered and managed. By modifying the prosthetic device by perhaps adding cushioning or padding this can help reduce pressure on the residual limb and joints thereby reducing pain. In my case having no residual limb, the socket I sit in needs to be cushioned for some degree of comfort. When new cushioning has been well-used, I do find it slowly compresses over time, which has a two-fold effect. Firstly it is not as comfortable, and secondly the height of the leg slowly reduces with more compression. This can increase pain and affects my walking style by making it more difficult and using more energy. It is only a small difference but that is all it takes to cause a progressive issue. In the past some sponge, covered by soft leather was used for my prosthesis but its properties soon changed and slowly degraded. Nowadays new materials in the marketplace appear regularly and are not just sponge-like materials but much more rigid in its form, yet compliant and longer lasting.

Some may not understand it, but psychological support can also play an important role in pain management. Support groups and other forms of psychological support can help amputees cope with the emotional and psychological impact of pain. It is important for new amputees to work closely with their healthcare providers to develop a comprehensive pain management plan which addresses the individual's unique needs and circumstances. With appropriate management and support, in particular family support, many amputees can effectively manage pain and enjoy a good quality of life.

In summary, the saying, 'no pain, no gain' is appropriate when starting to use a prosthesis and it can be a complete lifestyle change. Life is about change and how we manage it, and change happens when the pain of staying the same is greater than the pain of change. Embrace the change!

Jim - *Having an amputation performed is a real pain quite literally! In the U.S.A., medical people use a one to ten scale to have patients express their pain levels. A one is no pain, and a ten means you are 'blowing your brains out'. No two amputees experience pain and frequency the same way and to the same degree. On various amputee related social media resources the number one topic discussed is pain and its management. Some people report pain levels of two-three with others eleven-twelve!*

The two most common forms of an amputee's physical pain are 'Residual Pain' and 'Phantom Pain'. Residual pain is described as the pain which originates in the remaining part of your limb. It can be caused by a variety of conditions related to surgery or it can be caused by conditions prior to amputation. Phantom pain is described as ongoing painful sensations which seem to be coming from the part of the limb which is no longer there. The limb is gone, but the pain is real. In addition to physical pain, there is also emotional, psychological, self-worth and social regression pain which can be worse than physical pain. Phantom pain occurs in upwards of 80% of limb amputees.

I consider myself one of the luckiest amputees in the world. I experienced very minimal post-amputation pain and since then I have had no significant pain in the last five years. When I read the hundreds of posts of people suffering extreme pain and total disruption of their lives after surgery and reaching out desperately for help, I feel very sad and somewhat guilty. I think, "There but for the grace of God go I." There are the hundreds who reply on social media with all kinds of suggestions from lemon juice to CBD, to pharmaceuticals, heating pads and on and on goes the list. What works for one person may not work for another. It is trial and error.

I give all the credit for my pain free life to my wonderful "Good Doctor". I think one of the major reasons for being pain free was because my doctor included the Targeted Muscle Reinnervation (TMR) procedure with my amputation. TMR surgery is a surgical treatment which is gaining acceptance as a treatment for nerve pain associated with amputation. The surgical procedure is relatively new and until recently, surgeons performing amputations were not trained in how to do it. Word of its benefits is spreading rapidly, and many more surgeons are getting training to do it. Plastic surgeons were among the first to realise the benefits of TMR and many amputee surgeons bring in a plastic surgeon to do the procedure after the amputation is completed. Post-amputation pain is common among amputees. Some might feel sensations in part of the limb which remains after amputation or may experience phantom pain in the location of the amputation. TMR surgery can help reduce post-amputation nerve pain by reconnecting amputated nerves to nearby nerves and eventually muscle targets. Nerves are like electrical wiring with TMR helping to complete the "circuit" by reconnecting the "live wire."

The optimum time to have TMR Surgery performed is at the time of amputation. However, the surgery can be performed well after amputation. Many amputees who have struggled with phantom pain well after their amputation have had it done with success in significantly reducing or eliminating their pain. The shorter the timespan between amputation and TMR surgery, the better the odds for the procedure being successful. Like any other surgery, there are no guarantees every outcome will be 100% successful. Like any other solution, TMR might not be your solution for various reasons, but it is worth finding out if you are a potential candidate.

If you are facing an amputation, I would recommend discussing TMR with your doctor to determine if you qualify. If you are and your doctor is not qualified to do it and cannot bring in an associate to do it, I would consider getting another doctor.

There are all kinds of research being done for amputee pain management. The focus seems to be around the relationship between the brain, the nervous system, and the transmission of nerve impulses. Hopefully something even better than TMR will appear in the future.

Chapter 7:

Coping Strategies

It may seem strange how some people cope with being disabled because sometimes what others do would not work or even be considered by myself. Thank goodness we are all different though because many like to make a statement about their disability. For instance many amputees wear shorts and have their prosthesis showing without any fairing. Some even wear shorts not just in the summer but throughout winter too. I can understand how much easier the leg must be to take on and off, even for quick adjustments. If it works for them, then I am happy for them.

There is the flip side of the coin where some do not want to be seen in public as disabled and shrink into the background in a hermit like existence, shunning friends, and family. Again this suits some, but for most it is something not even considered. Us human beings are a social species which rely on cooperation to survive and thrive. Being alone or almost alone may have downstream consequences.

There is a uniqueness how each one of us copes with amputation and the differing factors influencing our reaction. Some grieve their loss, whilst others like me were relieved to rid themselves of something threatening their life. It does pose challenges on many levels which include physical, emotional, social, and spiritual. Emotional responses to amputation are different for every individual and their family. How people respond to their amputation depends upon their unique make-up and the meaning they give to their amputation. There is no one fit-all answer.

The age of the person affects how they will be able to cope psychologically, with children adapting faster than adults. The effects of amputation and how it relates to age are very complex and can greatly affect a person's life and ability to cope. The process of coping with an amputation begins long before the actual procedure, unless trauma is involved, and includes the family circle. It can be especially difficult for younger people who are less likely to have the capacity to process the implications of an amputation than those older. Regardless of age it is important they and their family receive appropriate emotional and psychological support from medical staff and others during this challenging time. When I was faced with amputation a long time ago there was hardly any support for me, and nothing for my parents or siblings. We just had to get on with it. How times, awareness and support availability has changed over the years, which is a real positive.

For adults and the elderly facing amputation it can change life as they know it. It is important for them to recognise the challenges ahead, such as the need to make lifestyle adjustments, changes in mobility, and physical capability, as well as psychological changes. Worries may arise over daily functioning, financial matters, and family relationships. Despite the difficulty of these changes the importance of finding coping strategies which will help them to adjust should be recognised. Grieving the loss of a limb can be a healthy part of the process and individuals should take the time to explore their feelings. This can be helped through peer support, therapy, and available mental health services.

When I had the appointment to try my first prosthesis on at seventeen years old, it was a little daunting, but I really wanted to have a leg to walk on again instead of using crutches, and my expectations were overly high. In those days there were a lot of World War II veterans there and they were mostly a jovial crowd who welcomed me into the 'amputee club'. There were also far more double leg amputees then than now.

For younger amputees the process of coping may differ considerably. Adapting to a physical change at a young age can be a difficult process and amputees may experience a wide range of emotions including shock, fear, guilt, and anger. Furthermore the physical challenges of learning how to use a prosthetic and how to adjust mobility and everyday life can be overwhelming. There is also the resilience of the human spirit in many where coping means to embrace what has happened and adjust accordingly to their new life. What should be remembered though is whatever the age, depression, anxiety, or post-traumatic stress disorder can happen after losing a limb.

Around the time of having an amputation it can help in acknowledging your feelings to heal and move through the grieving process. This requires something few of us do in looking inward at ourselves for self-examination of anger or sadness. It is far better to do this than suppress all the pent up emotional turmoil going on inside, which can boil over in unexpected ways, and is not a healthy alternative. It may require seeking help or even guidance from mental health professionals.

Negative emotions are very common and may include feelings of grief, sadness, anger, fear, guilt, and depression. They can be difficult to navigate and affect an individual's overall quality of life and mental health. Fears of the unknown, fear of pain, fear a prosthesis failing you, fear of not being able to cope, fear of dying, and fear of not being able to do activities which were possible before the amputation can make the adjustment process more difficult. One other negative emotion is depression, and it is a term used often when describing the experiences by amputees. Depression can manifest itself in a variety of ways and can range from mild to severe, it can also be long lasting and debilitating if not dealt with properly.

Depression can lead to a sense of isolation, and it is therefore important to keep contact with friends and family who can help lift spirits by being good listeners and encourage optimism. There are also nowadays many supportive groups of people who are going through or have gone through similar experiences. Just by sharing your experience with supportive people, you can learn new coping strategies and better understand your feelings. The adage of a trouble shared is a trouble halved comes to mind.

As an analogy, an amputation can be likened to retirement because you must embrace it. There is a mixture of feelings such as anxiety, anger and shock in some cases, depression, numbness, and a loss of sense of purpose to name a few. My wife's idea of a sense of purpose I believe was to make me a 'Retiree Apprentice' and to not tell me how long the apprenticeship is (although twenty-five years has been mentioned!). If this newfound purpose was to make me excited at the start of every day, then it has not quite worked but some other purpose would be beneficial. By having a purpose it is a way to lead a satisfying life, but in my case, housework and cooking does not provide this!

Although adjusting to life as an amputee can be difficult and challenging, setting meaningful goals can help work through the process and find a sense of fulfilment. Setting short term and long term goals can help to break this process into manageable pieces. Short term goals can be helpful in providing immediate relief and comfort. I have seen the joy of many over the years walking the rail length for the first time as they wear their prosthesis for instance. Other goals can include activities such as learning to eat with a prosthetic limb, attending church or support groups. When short term goals are achieved a sense of accomplishment is felt. Motivation and hope can help to move forward and continue to live life in a meaningful way. Long term goals provide an overall direction and help individuals strive for something bigger than just day-to-day activities. They give structure and purpose for the long term journey ahead. Long term goals should be achievable and realistic but should also challenge and push individuals so they can see the growth and progress in their lives.

One of my long term goals was to walk from the house where I lived to the nearby shopping centre and back, which was about a mile. I practiced walking and walking to achieve my goal but never made it. It was just too far away for me to manage. This was good for me to aim for something, which in the end was unachievable for me, but also the recognition I would not be able to do it. This is why realistic targets should be set and do not be too despondent if they cannot all be met. It is all part of the new journey you are on. Keep in mind, difficult roads often lead to beautiful destinations.

It is also important to build a support system as individuals pursue their goals, especially the older the person is. Family, friends, and healthcare professionals can help support amputees during this process. This can involve helping with the practical aspects of achieving goals as well as providing emotional support when achieving goals is difficult. Meaningful goals can help the process of adjustment to life with the loss of a limb and to help find a greater sense of purpose with short term and long term goals which are achievable while still providing a sense of challenge and growth.

By implementing a structured daily routine, new amputees can adjust more quickly and effectively to their new lives. It is also important to remember a daily routine should be tailored to the individual; the routine should not be too rigid and should provide enough structure and balance to help the individual manage the day-to-day tasks of their new life.

This structure and order are particularly helpful for those who have just experienced a significant change in their lives. A daily routine can help to stay focused and organised, allowing them to manage their daily tasks more easily. Additionally a routine can help reduce stress and anxiety levels, provide motivation to complete tasks, and provide a sense of security. Part of the anxiety build-up may be over concern for the anticipated reaction of loved ones and sympathy they receive. It is not an easy path to follow.

When creating a daily routine it is important to consider the individuals specific needs and abilities. It is also important to provide some flexibility and balance to the routine as well as ample time for rest or relaxation. Do be mindful of the individuals physical, and emotional needs as well as their mental health. As an example, a daily routine might involve getting up at a certain time or participating in physical activities. To keep the body healthy, attending regular medical appointments, and engaging in activities which promote social interaction with other amputees can help. Try also to include activities which are focused on positive thinking such as meditation, or mindfulness, because self-care is important.

For some, having a positive attitude in life is part and parcel of their being and extends to their new life as an amputee. I believe I have been fortunate regarding this. Many years ago when I was told I had a rare cancer, the consultant said to me there were only two cases a year in the UK, which at the time equated to odds of around 25,000,000:1. When someone asked how I felt about it, I immediately replied, 'Better me than anyone else.' It is a way of looking at events in your life, as traumatic and physically devastating as it may be. I have always believed it to be a healthy approach.

Keeping a positive attitude can help people cope with limb loss. I have done many things and met many people I would otherwise not have met but for my amputation. There is a need to focus on the things you can do and ways you have grown since the loss. Staying positive does not mean you need to ignore your feelings. There were some days when I had a young family, I wished I could be chasing them around the park or playing football with them. I knew this was a normal reaction so took a deep breath and did what I could by engaging in many other ways. After all the best thing you can give to the family is your time.

We are all different and our personalities react to limb loss in different ways. For example, people who tend to experience depression or anxiety may have more difficulty coping with limb loss than others. Likewise, highly self-reliant individuals might struggle more with amputation than someone comfortable with accepting help from others. The most important aspect is to focus on your strengths, try to embrace optimism and move forward in life.

For many facing the unknown, anxiety is a common side effect of an amputation or for any stressful, traumatic event. Anxiety is found moreso post-amputation and gradually declines as acceptance, and when a better understanding of what lies ahead is understood. Anxiety can relate to changes in body image, identity, and social roles. Those with anxiety might experience symptoms like insomnia, fear or worry, and if they persist some medical help may be required. By staying active, having social support, and endeavouring to be positive, all of these will help calm feelings of anxiousness.

There can be signs to look for if coping with the amputation is proving difficult, and this can come out in many ways. For some, certain coping styles or mechanisms do not work, and they are ineffective in dealing with stressful, difficult situations. These approaches are quite negative and may include avoidance, denial, blame, and numbing. For these styles of coping it can prove to be detrimental to an amputee as they often lead to increased psychological distress, depression, under, or oversleeping, anxiety, self-harm, and risk of suicide.

Often, they may be avoiding situations or people that make them feel uncomfortable. Denial is another bad coping style where they deny the reality of their condition and the impact it has on their life. Blaming themselves, or others is another bad coping sign. Numbing also means they may turn to alcohol, substance abuse, or other activities to numb the emotional pain of the condition. One other negative coping style found is where they allow themselves to depend on others beyond what is needed or even refuse to enter rehabilitation and demand a great level of care instead.

One strategy for overcoming this negativity is to identify mental health support services. Mental health professionals can provide counselling and other psychological treatments to help to learn to cope with the condition. Engaging in positive coping behaviours is another strategy, such as exercising, engaging in creating activities, and developing healthy eating habits. There is no one-fit-for-all solution to this healing process because each of us is unique. Therefore finding healthy ways to manage stress, anxiety and depression are important to find the right pathway for the new journey ahead.

I remember reading, "Sometimes the only way to the light is through the darkness, but there will be little beacons of light along the way which will help see you through. There is a duality of dark and light. Remember, we cannot shine without the dark." I thought this was quite relevant when learning to cope because behind those dark stormy clouds, the sun is always shining.

Jim - Working on this book has caused me to get my thoughts and feelings organised so I can effectively communicate how I think, feel, and act on each chapter.

Coping has not been a problem for me. Some days I cope better than others, but it has not been a major issue. Sometimes life will throw me a curve ball, but I have always figured out a way to deal with it.

I am a firm believer that everyone can control how they think about things. The brain is an infinite, empty space until we decide what to put in it. I choose to put positive thoughts in my space. My cup is always full - never half full or half empty. From my perspective, if your cup is only half full or empty, it means negative stuff can creep in to fill that empty half space. My cup has no room for anything other than positive thoughts. How do I keep my cup full? I talk to myself through silent thoughts and sometimes out loud. I usually do not talk to myself out loud around others or they might think I am crazy, and that is how I cope.

While much of my physical being has changed since my amputation five plus years ago, what has not changed is my understanding of who I am, and this has helped me cope. I still have the self-confidence, self-esteem, self-worth, value systems, positive attitude, sense of humour and other positive traits which I had prior to amputation. After reading many posts I mentioned earlier, I have come to the realisation most people who are struggling and have issues coping with their amputation have lost or question their characteristics I just mentioned. I would not criticise or find fault with anyone because all of us are different in how we try to cope with our individual situations. We are all unique.

Ageing plays a significant role in determining how we cope with all the issues related to our amputations. I am in my eighties but if I was forty or fifty years younger, my mindset toward my situation would be significantly different and I think I could still deal with it. Earning a living, raising a family, paying a mortgage, interacting socially and professionally with others to name a few would bring a different set of challenges into consideration. No question, it would be much more difficult to cope at those age levels.

Along with being self-dependent, the other best way I have found to be effective in coping with circumstances is to have a strong support system. It starts with family. Do everything you can to help your family understand what issues you are dealing with and enlist their help. Keep in mind this is all new to them as well and often they do not know what to do going forward. Communicate, extend yourself, reach out, ask for help, get out of your cave, be pro-active. I believe that people, by nature, are willing to help others if you communicate the help you need. I have asked family, friends and complete strangers for help hundreds of times and have never been turned down. I believe most people get personal satisfaction from helping someone.

Another key to coping is developing a "Herd Mentality". I recommend joining an 'Amputee Support Group'. Herd mentality is defined as the tendency of the people in a group to think and behave in ways that conform with others in the group rather than as individuals. There are hundreds of these groups all over the world with thousands of amputees willing to share information and just be there as someone who understands the problems you are facing. Practically everything I have learned about amputations has come from support groups and amputee specific social media.

My view is if you are coping with issues and need help and do not reach out, you have no one to blame but yourself.

Chapter 8:

Ongoing Care and Rehabilitation

Amputee's often face many challenges when it comes to their ongoing care and rehabilitation. There are numerous types of support available and various strategies to ensure successful care and rehabilitation.

The physical, psychological, social, and even spiritual aspects of care are all integral to the well-being of amputees. Physical care involves providing adaptive technology and a prosthesis to enable the amputee to function as normally as possible. Psychological care is necessary to help the individual cope with the trauma associated with limb loss and to learn how to emotionally process the changes which have occurred in their life and adjust to the new lifestyle. We are all different, with some accepting their newfound disability more easily than others whilst some struggling to accept it at all.

Social care provides support and education including working to dispel myths and stereotypes around amputee care. Spiritual care considers the many spiritual aspects of the individuals life including the role of faith in their life and the support offered by their religious or spiritual community. To some this can be a great sustenance.

It is possible to achieve physical, psychological, and emotional well-being through spiritual practises such as meditation and prayer as well as through connecting with the community of people who understand and empathise with the individuals experience. This connection with a supportive community can help to encourage positive feelings of self-worth, purpose, and acceptance. Additionally spiritual practises can provide a sense of peace and hopefulness by helping individuals define meaning and spiritual guidance in their lives.

I have known some believe it is the karma to go through amputation due to some past life misdemeanour. Others view it as part of the reincarnation process where lessons in life as an amputee must be experienced, and from that comes inner growth and understanding. In this way they grow spiritually.

Meditation and prayer can be a powerful tool for individuals with limb loss to find spiritual well-being through meditation. Individuals can access inner peace and clarity through prayer with some finding guidance and support from a higher power. It is also important to connect with the community which can offer support, understanding, and empathy. This could be a support group, a religious or spiritual organisation or any other source of community where individuals with limb loss can find a sense of belonging and acceptance.

In addition to prayer, meditation, and connecting with a supportive community there are other ways that individuals can promote their spiritual well-being. For example, writing, art, music, and other creative activities can be an outlet for self-expression which can help to increase a sense of satisfaction and fulfilment. I must admit when writing my autobiography there was a cathartic feeling and some release from doing it.

Practising mindfulness and being present in the moment can also help to promote spiritual well-being, as can engaging in physical activities such as yoga and where practical, walking. I do myself try to enjoy moments in the present and step back to savour them, knowing I am really enjoying that special moment rather than wait until later and reflect upon it.

Amputee spiritual well-being is an important area of care for individuals through utilising spiritual practises such as meditation and prayer. Connecting with a supportive community and engagement in creative activities individuals can access inner peace and find a sense of meaning and hope. It really is a case of what works for each of us.

Ongoing care for amputees is important because it allows them to receive dedicated support and resources from trained professionals on an ongoing basis. This bonding relationship can be quite effective and helpful. It helps amputees to better manage the physical, psychological, and social aspects of living without a limb. It also helps to keep them connected to their community which can be a source of strength and comfort.

There are several different types of services available to provide ongoing care. These include physical therapy, occupational therapy, psychological counselling, prosthetic fitting and rehabilitation, and spiritual care. All these services can help the amputee to better manage the physical, psychological, and social aspects of their life.

Assessing the ongoing care can be done through a variety of sources which include hospitals, clinics, and other healthcare facilities as well as government programmes, private organisations, and insurance companies. It is important to research these sources and to make sure the care provided is of the highest quality and suited to the individuals' specific needs.

The impact of an amputees ongoing care on an individual's life can be significant. People who receive ongoing care are better able to manage the physical, psychological, and social aspects of their life. This has been found to improve their self-esteem and sense of well-being, even some becoming more active in their communities. In addition, ongoing care can help to reduce the risk of depression, anxiety, and other emotional and mental health issues associated with living with limb loss.

Rehabilitation is an incredibly important part of the recovery process which helps adjust to the new reality and aids moving forward with their lives. It is not just physical recovery which is necessary but also psychological and emotional healing. Amputees must go through a process of learning how to live with their disability, how to interact with their body, and how to cope with the changes in their physical capabilities. This can be particularly daunting if the loss is through trauma because of the immediacy of it.

I remember shortly after my amputation, when I was still on crutches and outside my home, seeing an old school friend. I greeted him and he waved back but looked over his shoulder at me for several seconds in total disbelief, I thought. To me he seemed shocked to see me without my right leg. It was the look I still recall and the feeling of consternation and being overwhelmed by what he saw. That was fifty seven years ago but I recall it vividly. It is momenta like this where the adjustment to a new life, and new journey both psychologically and emotionally is not easy.

Rehabilitation can help amputees become comfortable with their new body and gain a renewed sense of self-esteem and confidence, in addition to physical rehab, amputees may also benefit from other forms of rehabilitation such as occupational therapy, vocational counselling, and psychological support. Occupational therapists help amputees adjust to their new physical abilities providing physical exercises and mobility training. Vocational counselling may help amputees identify and pursue meaningful career possibilities with their new physical limitations and psychologists can help to process their emotions and learn to cope with the trauma of their injury.

There are also support groups and resources available to help understand their condition and make informed decisions about their care and rehabilitation. This may cover not only their new limitations, but other opportunities not thought about or explored. Amputee Associations are a good source of information which can provide a sense of community and support to their members. There may also be financial resources available to help with medical bills and prosthetic expenses. These associations are often a hub of useful information and support.

Successful amputee rehabilitation can also benefit from lifestyle changes. Positive coping mechanisms such as exercise and healthy diet can help to improve physical well-being. Activities such as relaxation techniques can help reduce stress and support mental health.

In facing up to an amputation you cannot turn away from yourself forever because no matter where you go, you are always there. No matter what you do to avoid being yourself, you will always come back to having to face 'you' again. It is this acceptance which helps rehabilitation and recovery must come first so that everything you love in life does not have to come last.

In conclusion amputees face unique challenges when it comes to their ongoing care and rehabilitation. It is important for them to have access to physical, psychological, and emotional support services as well as to tap into available financial resources. Additionally lifestyle changes can help recover from their injury and move forward with their lives. It should also be remembered for some the rehabilitation to amputation, like losing a loved one, will take a lifetime. It does not matter how slowly you go, so long as you do not stop.

Jim - *This is the area of my amputee life that I have really messed up. I underestimated the amount of effort and physical training I should have done before and after amputation to prepare myself for life as an amputee. It has been verified lower limb amputees expend two and a half to three times more energy to walk than able-bodied people do. If you know you are going to have an amputation, my recommendation would be if you can, to get physically active and so get yourself in the best possible shape before amputation.*

After surgery, I spent two weeks in a rehabilitation hospital to give the residual limb time to heal and to work with PT's and OT's twice a day to build up my strength and balance. I was also measured for a custom-built wheelchair, and it was ordered. I was sent home with a loaner chair. I had a home health PT visit me three times a week to manage my ongoing exercise conditioning as well as a home health wound care nurse, who came twice a week to change my bandages.

It took about three months for my residual limb to heal completely with no complications such as pain or infection. Here again, I was blessed. I read the stories of those people who suffer with pain and infection in the healing process and feel badly for them. Do be sure you and your caregivers do everything you can to keep your limb clean and as infection-free as possible. There are limb protectors which can be used to protect your limb from physical injury. My incision closure is a work of art compared to pictures I have seen of other people's incisions. I recommend telling your surgeon you want a neat, clean, smooth incision closure to avoid any skin irritation issues when it comes time to getting a proper fitting prosthesis.

At this point is where I started to get off track. Since I had no knowledge of prosthetics, my doctor referred me to a company he had referred others to with some success. This became my first real lesson in understanding how the business of prosthetists works and problems encountered. I have Medicare and a supplemental insurance plan. They submitted my information to Medicare for approval to build my prosthesis. After four months of back and forth between the company and Medicare, it was finally approved. During that exacerbating period, without consciously realising it, I started slacking off on my physical exercises which was a big mistake. Running parallel to this was the slow paced Medicare approval and construction of my custom wheelchair. It took six months and reams of correspondence between my doctor and Medicare to convince them I need both a wheelchair and prosthesis. Meantime, I am waiting and avoiding doing my exercise program. My physical condition, which was not good in the first place was starting to atrophy.

My initial socket did not fit well and needed to be replaced which meant more time and exercise being lost. I went through three sockets with this company before switching to a different prosthetist. This required a new startup with Medicare and more time was lost and more atrophy happened.

Based on my personal experiences I make several points:

· The process of getting a proper prosthetic fit is difficult, frustrating and time consuming.

· Medicare and insurance companies move slowly, and I recommend pushing to keep the process moving forward.

· Despite time delays in the path of progress if your goal is to be mobile as much as possible, you need to stay focused on the goal of getting a well-fitting prothesis and not be satisfied until you do, regardless of how many prosthetists you need to use. I am on my fourth company in five years.

· Keep working on your physical conditioning regardless of delays and setbacks. It is essential to achieve your goal.

Rehabilitation is very complex. Once you are an amputee, you will be in a constant state of rehabilitation, some minor, some major for the rest of your life. Physical rehabilitation is just one part of it. The psychological, emotional, and spiritual rehabilitation aspects can be even more challenging than the physical. While there are resources out there to help you, how you handle all the multiple issues is up to you.

When all this "Amputation Stuff" starts piling up on me, I rearrange the issues to set priorities and what is important related to my amputee well-being. If you do not look at yourself objectively, seek help and resolve issues, it will bury you.

Chapter 9:

Social Isolation

Social isolation is a reality for many who are unfortunate to not have any family support, which may or may not be through choice. There are times when we all like our own space and enjoy the quietness of isolation and solitude, but this is for most short-lived and only wanted in small amounts of time.

For many amputees' social isolation is a serious issue which affects millions of people around the world. The trauma and long term effects of amputation can drastically affect the social life and mental health of individuals, leading to a feeling of loneliness and isolation. The physical and psychological effects can make it difficult or even impossible for them to participate in activities or interact with other people. The lack of physical mobility in activities can also lead to feelings of frustration and depression.

As we all get older our physical mobility gets less whether an amputee or not, but the onset of this reduced mobility is more pronounced if you are an amputee. The wear and tear on hip and knee joints having to compensate for a missing limb or two means the effects of ageing does come sooner rather than later. I know both my hip and knee require managing at times and I take pain and anti-inflammatory medication when needed. The invincibility felt as a young man to all this gradually turns into an acceptance of realism as the odd pain and ache becomes more and more pronounced and does not always go away. Some things you can change, some things you cannot change, and some things are a plain acceptance of where you are in life's cycle.

Depending on personal circumstances, ways of combating feelings of isolation and loneliness may include joining an online or in-person support group. This may include participating in activities which are adapted for those with physical disabilities. Also seeking professional help from a therapist or counsellor can be beneficial. Additionally family and friends can provide companionship, support, and understanding which can help the person feel more connected and engaged with the world.

Many people, not just amputees can experience social isolation for a variety of reasons. Focusing on amputees though, for some, the physical limitations of an amputation can make it difficult to participate in activities and engage with people. Lack of access to public transportation and specialised equipment for mobility can lead to further feelings of disconnection. In addition the experience of being an amputee can be a source of stigma and discrimination, creating feelings of alienation, shame and even depression.

Even wanting a taxi to take you somewhere can become a major obstacle especially if you need one with ramps which can take a wheelchair for instance. For me when I have visited London, I find getting into a black London cab is not as easy as a normal car. I have a hip lock which must be released when getting into the cab. I must hold my prosthesis under my thigh and place the leg inside the cab. It is quite an art to avoid not falling on the floor and you do need some good upper body strength to help do this and get in the cab. I always approach it with a sense of dread. This was in the past compounded if I was on a business trip with others, who got in first, and I had to follow. I found it somewhat embarrassing. Then there is the hailing of a cab because you cannot phone for one in the capital before the days of Uber, which at peak times can take an age. Meanwhile you are standing, waiting, and after twenty minutes or so the pain of standing starts to impact me. In one instance late at night when visiting London, we had to walk quite a distance to get to a main road before we could start to hail a cab. Small issues to most but significant if you are an amputee.

The physical and emotional impacts of amputation can create a sense of social isolation leading to a feeling of being cut off from the real world. This can be exacerbated by loneliness and poor self-esteem resulting in a feeling of exclusion from social activities and relationships. Nobody wants to be a burden to others but there is a degree of reliance on others, which impacts your own independence. There are ways amputees can cope with social isolation as we have described by participating in adaptive activities which can help to maintain independence and engage in physical activities.

Social isolation can occur at any stage of the amputation process from the moment of diagnosis to the days, weeks, and even years afterwards. Those who are newly diagnosed often struggle to find the right words to share their experiences and some may feel disconnected from their peers and family due to the physical and emotional changes they are going through. It is a traumatic time for everyone, including family and friends.

In the immediate days and weeks following the amputation, feelings of social isolation are often intensified due to the mobility and lifestyle changes in which a dawning of reality emerges. They may miss out on activities they used to enjoy with friends and face struggles such as learning to use prosthetic device, coping with medical appointments, and managing both physical and emotional pain. These difficulties can lead to feelings of loneliness and lack of connection with the world around them.

In the long term they may still endure a certain level of social isolation due to the unique physical and emotional challenges associated with their amputation. As their body has changed, they may no longer feel accepted by the family and peers which can lead to further isolation.

The feeling of isolation can be compounded by the lack of understanding and acceptance in society. They may feel like they are judged by those who may not understand the physical differences making it difficult to build meaningful relationships and form social connections. The lack of physical ability can also lead to a sense of inferiority and a lack of self-esteem because activities such as sports, hobbies, and travel may be difficult or impossible to participate in. In my case as a youngster I used to be in the cricket team, football team and was captain of the basketball team. I was physically quite active but had to readjust my expectations with a reality check on my new journey in life, following my amputation.

The stigma of amputees in society is a topic that has been largely overlooked in discussions about physical disabilities. Unfortunately this has resulted in a lack of understanding and empathy for those living with an amputation despite the advancements in modern medicine prosthetic technology. In recent years a real positive for society in general has been the Paralympics where achievements in the face of adversity through disability has raised much awareness worldwide. It will not happen overnight and people with physical disabilities are still often viewed with prejudice and discrimination though. This is especially true for amputees who face the added challenge of navigating the world with a visible disability.

The stigma of amputees can be attributed to several underlying causes including lack of knowledge and understanding of what an amputation is and how it can affect an individual's life. In some cases there may be a fear of the unknown or a general discomfort with physical differences. Additionally there are still many negative stereotypes and assumptions about those living with physical disabilities which can lead to prejudice and discrimination.

I was at a party recently talking to someone about my writing and the subject matter of my first book, which led to a discussion about my amputation and prosthesis. I explained I had lost my whole leg and part of my pelvis. She said she worked in a Care Home, and an old lady there had an artificial leg just above her knee. Every day she helped her to put her sleeve on and, then her leg on, and felt she was quite knowledgeable on the subject. I mentioned I went swimming while on my honeymoon in Tobago and she asked if I wore my leg in the water. I think this question to a hemipelvectomy about wearing a prosthesis in the water highlights the misunderstanding of my situation and lack of knowledge. She was a kind and caring lady, but like many saw an amputation of a limb as the same, no matter how much had been removed. It is about amputee education, but most people do not understand the issues, only those closest to us do.

This stigma faced by amputees can have a major impact on their quality of life. Those living with physical disabilities often feel isolated from society due to their visible differences. This isolation can cause feelings of loneliness and depression which can further perpetuate the stigma. Additionally many feel as though they cannot participate in activities or engage in social gatherings without feeling judged or out of place.

There are ways to counteract the stigma in societies by education and awareness campaigns which can be effective in helping to dispel myths and negative stereotypes. Increased visibility in the media can also help to destigmatize those with physical disabilities by providing positive representations. Finally more support services such as counsellors, support groups, and job training programmes can help to give amputees all they need to succeed in their daily lives. With this increased understanding they could then look forward to increased awareness and understanding for future acceptance and inclusion.

There can often be times in social isolation when reflecting on self-worth, but I read recently, "It is an absolute human certainty that no one can know his own beauty or perceive a sense of his own worth until it has been reflected back to him in the mirror of another loving, caring human being." What would we do without those wonderful people who help and tend us. They are and always will be to me the unsung heroes.

Jim - Since becoming an amputee I have not noticed any dramatic changes in my social interaction status and have not experienced any feelings of being isolated by my choice or by the behaviour of others. I believe we are the controllers of the decisions we make as situations arise in front of us. I posted my thoughts on a media site which stated: "I feel weird when I read threads like this one because in over five years, I have never experienced the negative reactions from "normal" people which some say they have experienced. Any interactions I have had with others have at worst case, been neutral and the majority are positive encounters. My theory is that a person's personality does not change from before amputation to after amputation. If you were an outgoing, sociable, positive thinker and good communicator prior to amputation, you are probably pretty much the same personality after amputation. Conversely, if you were an introvert, unsociable, withdrawn, negative thinker, poor communicator prior to amputation, you probably still have problems dealing with people. The only difference is now you have your amputation to use as a reason to justify why you think people are reacting to you the way they do. We owe it to ourselves and our fellow amputees to aggressively extend ourselves and educate those "normal" people about everything related to being an amputee. The more the public know about amputees, the better chance we gain support on issues to improve our lives."

I am not minimizing the point which many people do have with very real problems in social isolation after amputations. Friends desert them, spouses divorce them, careers are affected, finances shrink, and general mental and physical health suffers. If these events occur, seek help. There are hundreds of all kinds of support groups out there willing to help you, but you need to take the initial steps and make the effort to reach out to them and you will be welcomed with open arms. During my post-amputation rehab, an Amputee Coalition Support Group named "Lively Limbs" held their regular monthly meeting at the rehab hospital where I was. Out of curiosity, I attended and have been attending ever since. I have made numerous friends there and I became much more involved. Helping others is the best therapy for both the helper and those being helped. I believe the final stage of healing is using what happened to you to help others.

During my business career, my family moved seventeen times for my job-related positions. Twelve of those moves were with one company. We discovered we needed to take the initiative to meet people, make friends and interact with others. The same holds true with amputations. Generally, you need to make the first effort, take the first steps even if you are in a wheelchair, and reach out to others.

There are many other sources of support. Religious groups, veteran's groups, social media groups, special interest groups like sports teams, motorcycle clubs, are out there. I am always amazed by the number of biker amputees who cannot wait to ride again after losing a limb in an accident. I would suggest becoming an 'Amputee Advocate' and tell your story to people to help them understand what life as an amputee is all about. Like everything else in life, we have choices. You can say, "Oh woe is me" and stay isolated or you can accept the life-changing challenge to do everything you can to live your life as best you can. The choice is yours.

Chapter 10:

Mental Health

Mental health is an important consideration for people living with amputation. This applies both to pre and post-operation, including those longer term. The emotional effects of amputation can be profound and include feelings of grief, depression, and anxiety. I read about it constantly as a key thread on Social Media. It is important to remember access to mental health services and emotional support are key elements in providing quality care for amputees. Of course in this statement there is the consideration it may not always be available to everyone. It is a fact that each person may experience different levels of difficulty adjusting to life after amputation and should be provided with tailored support to help them cope with the emotional effects.

Grief is a natural emotion which amputees may experience after the loss of a limb. It can even happen pre-operation, if because of an illness it necessitates amputation. Grief can include feelings of sadness, shock, disbelief, guilt, anger, and helplessness. Experiencing these feelings is part of the healing process and can be dealt with in different ways depending on the individual. The support of family and friends is paramount and when necessary, seek the help of mental health professionals. Additionally there are support groups for amputees that can provide both emotional and practical support. I do think the social media groups provide a good service by enabling like-minded people who have similar experience offering help, support, and comfort at difficult times.

I have personally never suffered any grieving process, mainly because of the reason for losing my leg. The cancer in my leg was killing me and it needed to be removed. I could not grieve the loss of something so aggressive and life threatening to my being. It was quite the opposite, and therefore a relief to have it removed, as devastating physically as it was. I viewed it as the beginning of my new life's journey following the amputation. I think your mind-set plays a huge part in the recovery process and beyond which should never be under-estimated.

There is no doubt amputation can have a profound impact on an individual's mental health and needs to be addressed as part of a comprehensive treatment plan. Amputees are at greater risk of depression and anxiety. They may experience feelings of grief as described, including loss and trauma related to the amputation. Being such a new and unique experience to them it can be one of frustration and difficulty adjusting to the new physical limitations. On the other side of the coin are the new physical demands of walking especially in the older, more frail people. It can be challenging. Treatment for mental health disorders should be quickly identified to prevent further decline and complications.

Depression is a common issue among amputees and can be caused by a range of factors from physical and emotional adjustments, to changes in lifestyle relationships and overall outlook. Treatment for depression in amputees typically involves a combination of strategies such as medications, psychotherapy, lifestyle changes, and adaptive activities. The most relevant thing is to seek support from family, friends, and other amputees. I believe in talking to other amputees it may best suit someone with a similar type of amputation, whereby empathy is there straight away. There is much greater understanding of the issues involved if someone, say having a hemipelvectomy, talks to someone who has experienced this rather than a below knee amputation. I cannot emphasise this strongly enough as a good thing to do as this can be a source of inspiration and support. They will have first-hand experience on this issue or be able to recommend something constructive to move forward with. One effective way to help a lot is to just sit down and talk with someone who is neutral, on a one to one basis, without anyone else being present. Someone who does not know you and therefore have pre-conceived views on what is best for you.

I have been asked over the years by several prosthetists and physiotherapists if I would be willing to talk to other amputees who would appreciate advice or are struggling with the enormity of it. I do believe a sense of control and mastery of it helps enormously but this is easier said than done when someone is in a dark, lonely place. I would add in most cases it is often uplifting for me too in meeting like souls.

Body image and self-esteem are common struggles for many amputees with depression, often being linked to negative body image. It is important to focus on positive aspects of body image. Coping techniques such as relaxation, guided imagery, and positive self-talk can help boost self-esteem. Additionally engaging in activities which promote physical fitness and healthy social relationships can also aid in the development of a positive self-image.

Prosthetic devices can help with mobility and recovery however some amputees may feel self-conscious or have negative feelings about their appearance. My own experience is one of thinking I walk better than I do. I know I do this, and in doing some self-analysis of myself it must be my personal coping mechanism. It is one of the reasons I have not 100% accepted my disability. We too often look outward and not inward to try and understand the reasoning for our actions, emotions, and feelings. If you can do this, it can be rewarding and uplifting to explore.

It is necessary for amputees to learn and incorporate coping skills. I believe I did it sub-consciously because at the time, over fifty years ago, it was all new to me and nobody was available to guide or advise me. There is much help available and should be sought. Coping skills may include positive self-talk, mindfulness, relaxation techniques and seeking support from loved ones, including counselling. Many support groups are on social networking site on the internet and can be a real source of help and inspiration giving access around the world.

Social isolation can be common for amputees especially if they have difficulty with mobility or are hesitant to engage in social activities. It is sometimes a defence mechanism to withdraw into oneself rather than face the daunting prospect of a major life changing event. Most people whether able bodied or disabled dislike change and resist it. It stems from the interpretation of change as a threat and the body protects you with choices of fear, fight, or flight.

It can be challenging to keep up with former activities and relationships especially physical activities, even just walking or shopping with friends. My one thing I missed an awful lot was cycling but it is an adjustment which had to be made. Connecting with others through support groups, attending events hosted by local amputee associations, and joining online forums and discussion boards can help combat loneliness and promote a sense of community. It can also be beneficial to seek out mentors or role models who have had similar experiences and can provide insight into living within amputation. Engaging in activities that one enjoys and creating meaningful relationships with family members, friends and neighbours can greatly reduce feelings of social isolation. Socialising does not always equate to physical exertion. For instance I play a word game on my iPad and iPhone, like scrabble, with many people around the world, and over the years through interaction you do get to know them.

Rehabilitation and therapy are crucial components of care for amputees and include the use of prosthetics physical therapy, occupational therapy, and psychological counselling. Physical therapy helps amputees strengthen their muscles and improve their range of motion with exercises and stretches. Occupational therapy assists with activities of daily living and teachers the use of adaptive equipment. Psychological counselling provides support to amputees and their families as they adjust to their new physical reality. Using appropriate protective devices and proper body mechanics can help reduce the chance of re-injury and prevent chronic pain. Remember every prosthetic is bespoke because every amputee is unique.

By addressing physical limitations, particularly in the ageing population, rehabilitation and therapy can help improve an individual's self-esteem and quality of life by allowing them to adjust to their new body. The factor of declining mobility with age is strongly linked to a poorer quality of life. There is a definite reluctance amongst older amputees to use a prosthetic limb and this adds to their isolation.

We have previously mentioned the emotional and psychological trauma of losing a limb which can be difficult and an overwhelming experience. Although we may think of war veterans suffering post-traumatic stress disorder (PTSD) following their injury, it can happen to anyone in everyday life if the reason is traumatic and not just in a conflict situation.

PTSD appears to be more common in amputees following combat, accidental injury, burn, and suicide attempts. In contrast it is relatively rare among amputees whose surgery follows a chronic illness.

Symptoms of PTSD in amputees include fear, anxiety, depression, nightmares, flashbacks, and avoidance of situations that may remind them of their loss. There are several possible triggers of PTSD in amputees, from the physical loss of the limb to the trauma of experiencing a traumatic event, to the psychological stress of adapting to life with a physical disability.

Treatment for amputee PTSD typically involves a combination of psychotherapy, CBT (cognitive behavioural therapy), support groups, and medications. Psychotherapy helps amputees process their feelings about their loss, address feelings of guilt and sadness, and learn more healthy coping mechanisms. It can also give you a better understanding of the triggers causing it. CBT helps amputees learn to manage their fears by recognising and re framing their negative thoughts. Support groups again offer a sense of community and provide emotional support. Medications such as antidepressants, anxiolytics, and antipsychotics may also be prescribed to help manage symptoms of PTSD. The anxiolytic drugs treat symptoms of anxiety such as feelings of fear, dread, uneasiness, and muscle tightness which may occur as a reaction to stress. Most anxiolytics block the action of certain chemicals in the nervous system. The antipsychotic drugs are a type of psychiatric medication which are available on prescription to treat psychosis. Symptoms in extreme cases would include psychotic experiences or schizophrenia.

For amputees there are also lifestyle changes and adaptive strategies that can be used to help cope with PTSD. This includes things like proper nutrition, regular exercise, and engaging in activities that bring fun and purpose. Additionally amputees can also consider talking to a mental health professional for further support. The quality of life for everyone is an important factor of wellbeing but this can be affected by ageing and mental health issues. Pain and other physical ailments exacerbate these issues and underline the importance of ongoing care and rehabilitation.

In older war veterans, studies have shown the prevalence of PTSD can be double those suffering from depression. The transition to life with a disability can be difficult and challenging but with the right strategies and professional help it is possible for amputees to manage the emotional and psychological distress associated with PTSD.

Amputees dealing with PTSD or phantom pains often turn to drugs and alcohol to self-medicate to cope with the intense emotions and distress associated with this condition. Whilst this is an understandable impulse it is also highly dangerous and can have devastating consequences both short and long term to both physical and mental health. Among older war veterans they often show a lack of engagement with the potential psychological consequences of traumatic limb loss. There is an almost stoic view of being able to cope without anyone's help. The obvious and easily stated remedy is to find healthier alternatives to drugs and alcohol, but this is a simplistic statement to make when dependency is high.

The immediate reaction to the news of amputation depends on whether the amputation was planned, occurred within the context of chronic medical illness, or was necessitated by a sudden onset of infection or trauma. The psychological reaction to amputation varies significantly from person to person. Generally individuals who experience amputation may experience shock, disbelief, sadness, distress, and anger. I have personally known people to just give up and believe their life is over. Anxiety may be around the fate of the limb that will be removed, as well as about the prospect of phantom limb pain, which many may be familiar with.

As they adjust to their new body, they may also feel disconnected from their body and have difficulties adjusting to their new identity. This can lead to feelings of isolation and depression. Additionally individuals may experience physical pain, nightmares, flashbacks, and intrusive thoughts related to the traumatic event. They may even have difficulties with activities of daily living such as getting dressed, eating, and bathing. Professional help needs to be sought as soon as possible to manage these psychological difficulties.

Mental health problems can emerge through a complicated series of psychosomatic disorders in response to a limb loss. This is a psychological condition involving the occurrence of physical symptoms but usually lacking any medical explanation. What it does is affect their ability to function well. The other response is called somatopsychic disorder, which is again is a mental disorder exacerbated by somatic disorders. This is when a person's focus on pain or weakness for instance is excessive causing normal functioning to be a problem. Many general medical conditions are recognised as causing psychiatric symptoms, in particular amputation, but medical knowledge in this field is still expanding.

Studies appear to show that amputees are more likely to suffer from dementia than those able bodied. The factors believed to contribute to this are the underlying physical and psychological effects and can be associated with the amputation. Changes such as the physical functioning, increased vulnerability to cardiovascular and metabolic diseases, depression, and social isolation are all contributary.

Dementia can cause significant changes in an individual's mental health and cognition which impairs their ability to think, communicate, and perform daily activities. It is important for those living with an amputation to be aware of the potential for an increased risk of developing dementia and take steps to minimise the risk. Some of the ways which individuals living with an amputation can reduce their risk of developing dementia include staying socially active and engage in exercising regularly, eating a balanced diet, and seeking treatment for any underlying physical or mental health conditions. Additional therapy such as cognitive stimulation, physical activity, and music therapy can help individuals to maintain cognitive function. To me as an ageing amputee, a lot of this is just normal living but for others with reduced physical ability, dealing with other physical or mental health issues it can be daunting.

Fellow amputees should also pay close attention to any changes they may be noticing in their memory or thinking, and to talk to their doctor if they have any concerns. Early diagnosis and treatment of dementia can help to slow the progression of the disease. This of course applies to anyone whether disabled through amputation or not. By taking these steps, individuals can reduce their risk of developing dementia and increase their expectancy of life and mental well-being.

It is important when dealing with mental health to be patient in trying to understand what is happening to the person. I read; mental health problems do not define who you are. They are something you experience. You walk in the rain, you feel the rain, but you are not the rain.

Jim – *There is no question that all aspects of our life change and become more complex and challenging when our amputation occurs. Additionally, the lives of those in direct contact with us dramatically change as well. While physical, emotional, social, and financial health issues are important, our mental health sets the stage for dealing with how we manage our lives as amputees. All our various health issues are constantly interacting with each other. Our mental state at any given time determines how well we manage them.*

I cannot tell anyone how to manage their mental health or any of the other issues. What I can tell them is what works, or does not work, for me.

Maintain a 'Positive Attitude.' *In 1637, Philosopher Rene Descartes' wrote "Cogito, ergo sum". "I think, therefore I am." My personal interpretation of that statement for use in my own mental health world is, "I am who I think I am." I think of myself as a positive thinking person. I try to act positively in everything I do, especially in my interactions with others. I passionately believe in the "Rub-off effect." If we create an aura of positivity around us, it will rub off on others and then bounce back to us. It is a back-and-forth tennis match using positivity as the tennis ball.*

Use 'Creative Thinking' *to help find solutions to issues. The simple task of dressing can be an issue. I saw a video of a legless young man in a business suit who was leaving work in his wheelchair. He wheeled up to the back of his BMW SUV, electronically opened the hatch, and hopped out of his chair onto the back deck of the SUV. He then pulled his chair up onto the deck, closed the hatch then crawled over the back seat. He then crawled over and into the driver's seat, buckled up, activated the car and his hand controls, and drove off. That is creative thinking.*

Help Others. *All amputees need help. Do not isolate yourself. Get involved and get out of yourself. You will feel better and so will they. There are options on the internet. Join a 'Support Group' by virtual Zoom-type meetings or in-person meetings as well as 'Support Groups,' seek professional help when needed. Be empathetic and build rapport with others without joining the 'Pity Parties.'*

Ignore the Negative World. *I try to vigorously avoid news broadcasts and other negative web sites, TV, and radio programming. It is exceedingly difficult to do but I try because for me it just drags you into a hell hole.*

Smile and Laugh. *It is true, laughter is the best medicine. Every morning, I look at myself in the mirror and smile for a while. I make funny faces to stretch my facial muscles so smiling will be easier the rest of the day. Try it! It sets the tone for the rest of your day. Smile at everyone you meet because it is infectious. When we moved into our assisted living facility, I started smiling at everyone because very few people were smiling. Now, four years later when people see me coming, they start smiling even before I do. I love to tell jokes. I do it every chance I get because I love to make people smile and laugh. There is even scientific evidence that smiling promotes health.*

Ten big benefits of smiling:

1. *Smiling relieves stress.*
2. *Smiling elevates your mood.*
3. *Smiling is contagious.*
4. *Smiling boosts the immune system.*
5. *Smiling may lower blood pressure.*
6. *Smiling reduces pain.*
7. *Smiling makes you attractive.*
8. *Smiling suggests success.*
9. *Smiling helps you stay positive.*
10. *Smiling helps you live longer.*

Source: www.verywellmind.com

Chapter 11:

Relationships

Relationships are complex and for many, meaningful and supportive. In any crisis in your life, be it medical, like an amputation or loss of someone close, the support given can be invaluable. I know from personal experience how losing my first wife through cancer it helped tremendously to cope with the support and help I received from family and friends. Likewise having my amputation at sixteen was extremely difficult, but my family were always there and supportive.

From my perspective the two most important things in life are your health and family, in whichever order you want. You need family if there are health issues, and you need your health to support the family.

There are best described four types of relationships: Family, Friends, Acquaintances and Romantic. In each there is a connection, association or involvement which brings many aspects to enrich our lives. The healthy relationship brings trust, respect, open communication and most importantly honesty. All these relationships are interpersonal with those closest to you and fulfil a range of physical and emotional needs. It can be said there is some kind of interpersonal relationship with everyone we know.

To have a healthy relationship requires two-way conversations. We all have good and bad days, and if we are going through some trauma then the conversation is not always evenly balanced because of other aspects at play. Communication is essential and it is both important to listen and be heard. How often do you see someone trying to communicate but not actually listening. Or after you have spoken, they say, 'Yes, but...... They just want to get their point of view across and are closed to the others point of view. Maybe we are all guilty of this at times. Not listening is not healthy in a relationship.

How often do we say to someone, 'How are you today', not really expecting anything other than a response saying. 'I am fine, thank you'. Perhaps if the person being addressed looks, or is troubled, then add, 'No! How are you really feeling right now!', which might get a meaningful response or just thought be provoking for the individual. The conversation must be two-way though; hence the relationship needs to be healthy. There is also trust involved, especially if sharing some intimate details not to be repeated, therefore trust must come into play. Of course there is nothing wrong in disagreeing and respecting a difference of opinion without becoming too irate. I know sometimes rather than prolong or get into a heated argument it can be best to agree to disagree, while still respecting their view because everyone is entitled to their opinion.

Having an amputation, or as ageing takes its toll on you, can in some instances strain relationships, especially if communication is one sided. The closeness you feel with family and friends is an important part of social support and is also built on loyalty and trust. To be successful it cannot be one sided to be healthy. It is important to establish boundaries of communication especially as some people are and want to be private. Being respectful, but above all by being a good listener will help enormously.

When having dialogue with someone after an amputation it is best to have a positive attitude but be mindful and realistic about what you are saying. When I lost my first wife, one thing said to me was, 'Time is a great healer'. I did not like that saying because you do not heal with time, you just adjust to your loss for the rest of your life. It still grates with me when I hear anyone using that saying. Be mindful of jokes too, especially about amputees. At the time they may be laughed at but not everyone appreciates the joke after the raw experience of amputation. They may laugh to spare any embarrassment to both parties but be wary!

Not every partner can cope with an amputation especially if the relationship was not strong in the first place. The major struggle is communication. There is so much disruption around surgery and post-surgery, with emotions and physical well-being stretched to its limit at times. There can be sensitivity as to what to say or even saying the wrong thing in case the new amputee's fragile self-esteem is shattered.

Most do not plan for amputation and all the emotional stress involved with potentially shifting roles in their relationship, which is unplanned, change. If communication is not happening from either partner, then understanding feelings and mood swings can cause real tension to the detriment of the relationship. There can even be a feeling of never being able to understand what it feels like to be an amputee, so why talk about it. 'They were able-bodied, but I am disabled, and they just do not understand' is one quote. This new status of being disabled can make the person too proud or afraid to even ask for help and this reflects on poor communication, which in the end sours the relationship.

For relationships to survive, both partners must be willing to be honest with each other and talk without blame or accusation. One thing sometimes forgotten, but so important, is the partner is also experiencing their own post-amputation grief too. Everyone is focused on the amputee but there is a major impact on the other half too. Their whole world has crumbled, and they must be both emotionally and physically strong. It can be a traumatic roller coaster of weeks, months, even years of taking the blows but still trying to remain on track. Sometimes being totally honest, as painful as it is can be, is a good thing even if it hurts the other person. Sugar coating issues is not always the best way, and as the saying goes, 'Honesty is the best policy'.

Relationships can therefore be affected in various ways for amputees:

- **Self-esteem**: Amputees may struggle with body image issues and self-confidence, especially if they feel self-conscious about their amputation. This can affect their ability to form and maintain healthy relationships.

  Amputation can cause changes in a person's body image which can be difficult to adjust to. The absence of a limb can make the person feel different or unattractive and self-conscious. Loss of some degree of independence in which they may need help with tasks they previously did on their own may affect their self-esteem.

  There are also negative social attitudes to deal with because some people still hold negative attitudes toward those with amputations, seeing them as odd, or abnormal, creating a social stigma. Nowadays there is much more acceptance of disability, and it is embraced much more by society than ever before. The Invictus games have educated many in society and shown what individual strengths those with disabilities have and what they can still achieve. I have personally seen a positive step change in this over the last fifty years.

If amputation is the result of a severe injury or illness it may have been a traumatic experience, and trauma can affect a person's self-esteem making them feel vulnerable or powerless. People with amputations are also at an increased risk of depression which can cause feelings of hopelessness, low self-worth, or a lack of motivation. In this case it may need more than just family support, and medical advice may be needed.

- **Intimacy**: Depending on the level and type of amputation, amputees may have physical limitations or difficulties that can make sexual intimacy challenging or uncomfortable. This can put a strain on romantic relationships.

Intimacy can for many be a sensitive and difficult topic for individuals who have recently undergone an amputation. It is important to remember that each person's experience and feelings towards intimacy may differ, and their physical and emotional needs should be respected. As people age, their sex-drive often reduces and may stop entirely. In a loving relationship this is acceptable by both partners and does not become an issue.

There are however several ways to address these intimacy issues, such as encouraging open communication with your partner. Ask them how they feel about intimacy, or physical contact, and their comfort level in even discussing it. Be patient and understanding by listening to their concerns. Educate yourself about the physical changes that may have occurred due to the amputation. This can help you to be more understanding of their needs and concerns.

Be open to experimentation in trying new positions or ways of being intimate which is both pleasurable and comfortable. It needs to work for both of you and may require some experimentation and creativity, which of course may be fun too. It is not necessary to go out immediately and buy the Kama Sutra but gently approach what is best for the both of you. A sense of humour will always help! The saying, 'If at first you don't succeed then try, try, and try again,' springs to mind!

There is also professional support to be sought. This is not something which is new because people have been dealing with these issues for centuries. Encourage your partner to seek professional support from a therapist or counsellor if issues persist. These specialise in working with individuals who have had amputations. It may help to better cope with the emotional and physical changes which come with amputation.

- **Social stigma**: Unfortunately some people may still hold negative attitudes towards amputees, which can affect their relationships. For example a partner may feel embarrassed or ashamed to be seen in public with an amputee.

Social stigma attached to being an amputee can lead to discrimination and prejudice. Many people with amputations face challenges in their daily lives due to the negative attitudes and perceptions of others. One of the main issues with the social stigma of being an amputee is the assumption that individuals with disabilities are not capable of living a full and fulfilling life. This can lead to feelings of inadequacy, self-doubt, and anxiety. Moreover this stigma can also affect the social relationships, prospects, and access to public spaces. This is such an archaic viewpoint which can take generations to shift the uneducated bias which still exists in some form, even today.

It is therefore incumbent on us to raise awareness and educate the public about the capabilities and strengths of people with disabilities, including amputees. Through this we can work towards breaking down the social barriers, promote inclusion, and create a more accepting and inclusive society for everyone.

- **Dependence**: Amputees may need extra support and assistance from their partners in daily tasks, such as getting dressed or doing household chores. This can create feelings of dependence which may be overwhelming or stressful for both parties.

Various activities of daily living, especially if they have lost a limb or multiple limbs can be quite difficult after amputation. This dependence can be temporary or permanent and it is often related to the type and level of amputation, the physical condition of the individual, the age of the person, and the availability of support systems. It is a learning process after amputation of what you can do or what you hope to do, recognising what you would like and may never be able to do. This is a form of acceptance of your new self and promotes a realistic outlook.

I know how fortunate I am to have a wife who always puts me first, as I try hard to do for her. Little things she does daily without thinking to make my life easier, many unsaid, but many noticed. My life would be more difficult without her, and I cannot ever imagine my life without being together. I have been blessed.

I do remember the high expectations I placed upon myself once I had my prosthetic and how far I would be able to walk. The pain and exertion required by me to walk soon turned my expectation into realism. As much as I tried to be pragmatic, my expectations were tempered with what I could do, without overdoing things, causing problems and the consequences of that.

Someone who has had a below knee amputation may initially need help with activities such as putting on shoes, whereas someone with above the knee amputation may require more extensive assistance with personal care, mobility, and transportation. It is down to each individual and their mobility, age and health or any underlying health issues. Additionally people who have lost their dominant arm or hand may find it challenging to perform tasks such as writing, cooking, or driving.

Dependence on others does not necessarily mean that amputees are helpless or incapable. I personally need very little help, but my wife may disagree! What she does are simple things to save me walking, and it is always appreciated. With appropriate rehabilitation and assistive devices, such as prosthetics, wheelchairs and orthotics, many amputees can achieve a level of independence, and lead a fulfilling life. It is essential to provide support and education to amputees and their families by empowering them to improve their quality of life and achieve their goals. Do try and be realistic with the goals and aim for the moon but be happy if you hit the top of the telegraph pole.

- **Communication**: Amputees may need to communicate their needs and limitations clearly to their partners, which can require open and honest communication this can be challenging if one or both parties are not used to talking about difficult topics.

To be fruitful and meaningful any communication is best two-way. It may sound like an obvious thing to point out but most of us are guilty of paying lip service to conversations if we are otherwise distracted. I know if I am reading a paper or watching a television programme and my wife starts talking to me, I might find it difficult to shift my attention away and just hope I say, 'Yes or no', in the right place or context.

By refreshing ourselves in the etiquette of communication, the following prompts may help when talking to someone who is a recent amputee. Ask any questions in an open-ended way to try and really understand how they are feeling. It is important to respect their independence and be kind while they work out how to do something. Try to use simple language to express your thoughts, feelings, and questions rather than trying to be subtle and not getting a meaningful response.

One of the put-downs, which personally grates with me is using patronising language and allowing assumptions to creep in. If you are not an amputee, you cannot know what someone has or is going through. You can empathise but avoid patronising, especially understanding of their physical and emotional needs.

If your open questions lead to conversation, let them take the lead so they can express themselves. In doing this it helps them to understand their own issues and may even prove to be cathartic. Do not force help on them, just offer it. Try to empathise with any adjustments they have had to make in their life because of their amputation. As the saying goes, 'A trouble shared is a trouble halved'.

Losing a limb or even more than one, whichever way you look at it, or experience it, is traumatic at any age. I have often thought to myself having lost my leg at sixteen, what the 'best' age is to have an amputation. I might add, I use the word 'best' lightly. It is difficult to say perhaps what the 'worst' age is to have an amputation as each individual experiences the physical and psychological effects of amputation differently. What is important is to provide support, advocacy, and resources to those who are facing an amputation regardless of their age.

There are all sorts of reasons various age ranges come into play but to turn it on its head I would change the question to, 'What is the 'worst' age to have an amputation? My personal response is later in life and rising exponentially as the age gets higher. Having experienced life as an able bodied person and faced with the physical and emotional trauma it can be daunting. This in later life can be compounded if other health issues come into the equation.

As all of us age and none of us know how long our life span is going to be. If you have been fortunate to have lived a long life when amputation arises there is less certainty of more years than in a younger person. I have seen it in the raw when aged people at the Enablement Centre I attend for my prosthesis repairs attend for their first fitting of a prosthetic. Physically they may be struggling let alone emotionally with those first few steps on a new prosthesis and it can take a real toll.

Strength in your body to compensate for limb loss is quite important. Just getting up from a chair requires arm strength if leg muscles are missing. The body does compensate but it needs working on and does not just happen, it takes effort and time.

Amputation recovery takes longer, relative to age, with patience and understanding needed in abundance. The way forward is to have a positive outlook through positive dialogue, and this should be encouraged with all new amputees. Overall, relationships can be affected in many ways for amputees but with patience, understanding, and empathy, most challenges can be overcome. We just need to learn how to develop and maintain them.

In the wider circle of relationships the friends and family may go through many of the same feelings the amputee is experiencing. This helps when the dialogue is clear and unambiguous with them and their social support networks. In cases of trauma there are at play many aspects including protecting the amputee where discussion with a psychological therapist may be beneficial. Others may benefit from a confidential place in which to share their concerns because confidentiality becomes critical when working with an amputee, friends and relatives, and information should not be shared without consent.

Always be mindful in a relationship, the one thing to hold onto is each other.

Jim - There are so many variables to this subject that it is hard to decide where to begin. Like others, my primary relationships revolve around my family. My wife and I were high school sweethearts and we have been married over sixty-five years. Despite major difficulties we all experience, we have all stuck together as a family unit when compared to what has happened to the family structure in America and other countries in the last fifty years or so. We have worked hard at creating and maintaining the bonds which hold our family together.

There is no question that an amputation puts an unexpected and unplanned significant strain on a family. There is the initial shock when the amputation happens and then there is a lifetime of issues dealing with this by the amputee as well as all those in the amputee's circle of family and friends. We had been married for sixty years when I had my amputation and managing serious issues was not as traumatic for us since we already had been through other challenging medical, financial, and personal situations. Believe me when I say my wife has already had her one-way ticket to heaven punched! Our children had left the nest years before and while they and their families have been incredibly supportive, regular direct contact with me is difficult because of where they live, and they are busy with raising their families. I strongly empathise with younger families who are struggling with issues as I communicate and try to support them through social media sites.

I do not have what I would call strong friendships. During my business career, we moved our family a considerable number of times all over the Eastern United States. We have lived in six states and finally retired in Arizona; we also moved within those states more than once. Seventeen times in total. As a result, we never lived anywhere long enough where we had an opportunity to develop strong, long-lasting friendships. We developed a sizable number of friendships and acquaintances but over time and distance, those tended to drift away. While I would love to have a larger base of friends, I understand why the situation is what it is. I realise they come from large families or have close friends as part of their life, which leads me to my next point.

Who has the primary responsibility for managing, maintaining, and growing relationships after amputation with family and friends? The simple answer is you do! As an Amputee, you have two choices. You can disconnect yourself from family and friends, crawl into a hole and disappear or you can take a cheerful outlook, leadership role and extend yourself to family and friends. Keep in mind this is all new to them too. As human beings, they do not know how to react and tend to back away from situations which they are not familiar with or know about or even understand. In my view it is your job to educate them, help them understand what you are dealing with, help them realise you are the same person you always were minus parts. Communicate with them and let them know how you feel. When you focus on problems, you will have more *problems. When you focus on the possibilities, you will have more opportunities.*

Use every source you can find to educate yourself and others. Join support groups and use social media support groups. The more you extend yourself with a cheerful outlook, the better your chances will be of building stronger relationships with friends and family. No one has a better understanding of what being an amputee is all about than another amputee.

Chapter 12:

Cost of Caring

When we look at the cost of caring, firstly the monetary value springs to mind but there are other costs in many numerous ways which should be explored, understood, and even cherished.

The cost of caring for amputees can be high both financially and emotionally. The costs associated with amputation depending on your location can include medical bills for the surgery, prosthesis, rehabilitative care, and follow up visits as well as modifications to the home or other living spaces. Additionally they may need to purchase specialised equipment and supplies to help them manage daily activities. Physical and emotional costs can also be significant and include pain and rehabilitation, as well as mental and emotional stress caused by the trauma of limb loss. Sometimes when reading about how others must cope, I am truly grateful for the National Health Service here in the UK.

On the financial side there are several government programmes. If we look at the USA for instance, there is aid including the Social Security Administration Department of Veterans Affairs and Medicaid. These programmes can help to cover medical and other expenses associated with amputation, additionally many charities and non-profit organisations such as the Amputee Coalition offer support and assistance to amputees by providing resources, information, and financial aid.

A friend of mine in Belize, Central America offers weekly free help to the local people, and in conversation with him, he said a young girl who had a hemipelvectomy, like me, has been unable to afford a prosthesis and has been using crutches for the past ten years. We should all count ourselves lucky at times because our situation could be far bleaker especially just thinking of some of the war torn areas in the Middle East.

For those without access to these resources, amputees may need to rely on their own financial support as well as private loans and donations. Accepting help from friends and family can be beneficial as these individuals can provide emotional support and assistance with daily tasks. Although some may find this difficult to accept for their own self-esteem, they need to consider the human spirit of giving and the good people doing this for them. Again I say there is more pleasure in giving than receiving. The most important thing for amputees to remember is that adapting and coping with life after limb loss is ultimately a personal journey and cost should not be the biggest factor in determining their quality of life.

The emotional cost of caring for amputees may be one of the most overlooked considerations in the process of adjusting to limb loss. The psychological and emotional impact of amputation can be debilitating and cause a variety of challenges for not only the amputee but also for those in their support system, family, and friends. Helpers of an amputee may struggle with providing the necessary emotional support, in addition to the physical care that is often required. This can be a significant burden for those providing emotional care as they are often faced with challenges they may never have anticipated and have no experience of. There is little or no training yet suddenly they are thrust into a new world whilst possibly still reeling from the loved one's amputation trauma.

In the UK for instance there is a Carers Allowance given to financially help disabled people, but once retirement is reached the allowance stops. I assume because the statutory pension payment commences, and many feel the effects of reduced income to the family home.

The emotional care of an amputee is paramount to their continued well-being and successful adaption to their new circumstances. They may feel overwhelmed, frustrated and even hopeless in the wake of their limb loss, intermingled with phantom pains and the frustration of lack of mobility. It is essential they have individuals in their lives who can understand and empathise with their experience. Emotional support can be offered through conversations, listening, understanding, and encouragement. It is important to remember that each amputee will have different needs and it is important not to make assumptions about what they need.

The financial cost of caring for an amputee can be considerable. The prosthetics that are often necessary can be expensive if you are not in the National Health with the additional medical cost adding up quickly. Fortunately there are many resources that can provide financial support for amputees including charitable organisations, private loans, and donations. However even with the help of these resources, amputees may still be faced with financial hardship, especially if they have been the breadwinner for the family. It really can be a whirlpool of emotions with worry about the future not far from the top of the list.

In addition to the physical and financial implications, caring for an amputee has an emotional cost as well. Caring for a family member or close friend can lead to feelings of sadness, anger, and guilt. It is also common for carers to fill overwhelmed and exhausted by the demands of caring for an amputee. These emotions can be intense, and it is vital helpers take time to care for themselves as well.

Caring for an amputee spouse can be a challenging and difficult experience but it is possible to create a successful loving marriage despite the added emotional and physical costs of the situation. Amputee marriages are more likely to succeed when both parties are fully committed to placing their marriage and the needs of their spouse first. This means being willing to set aside any personal desires to focus on the needs of the amputee and the relationship. Like any marriage it will work if you both put yourself last.

To have a successful amputee marriage both partners must have realistic expectations about the physical and emotional costs of the situation and be willing to make sacrifices to help their spouse cope with the changes brought on by the loss of a limb. It is important for the couple to have an open and honest communication about their needs, goals, and expectations, and to be sensitive to the unique struggles their partner is facing. To me the successful marriage is one where communication is an everyday part of living together. As an aside, I tell my wife her tongue is afraid of the dark, and her usual retort is that I look better in the dark too. Humour certainly helps!

It is also crucial for the non-amputee spouse to be supportive of the amputee and to understand the feelings of grief, depression, and frustration are common and normal. They should not be taken personally. Providing consistent emotional care and encouragement is vital for the amputee to help them cope with and adjust to the changes in their life. This can also bring both parties closer together creating an even stronger bond.

I remember when I was in London having my amputation operation and my mother visited me every day. This journey took over an hour by two buses to get from where she was staying. I was always pleased to see her but had so little strength because the cancer had taken it from me. I remember saying more than once, after a few minutes, for her to go. I did not have the strength to talk much. She never left but always stayed. It probably hurt her my saying that. This is an example of unconditional love a mother has for a child, and likewise a spouse has too.

On one of the media groups it is apparent there is much love for many going through this trauma but there are others where the overwhelming change in circumstance is too much, and the relationship ends. Not everyone can cope or even put others before themselves. We are all different and it is easy to look at what happens and make judgement, but unless it has been experienced personally, the full impact cannot be judged. The relationship before events unfolded may not have been good to begin with so do not be too harsh in any criticism.

The emotional cost of caring for an amputee can be considerable but it is a necessary part of helping someone adjust to a life with the loss of limb. The most important thing for those providing care is to always make sure the amputees needs are met and remember everyone's experience with limb loss is unique. Providing emotional support and understanding can make a tremendous difference in their adjustment and quality of life.

The cost of caring for an amputee can be extensive, ranging from medical bills to assistive devices and psychological support. The non-amputee spouse should be prepared to take on much of the financial burden of their amputee partner's care. They may also need to provide extra emotional and physical support as the amputee will likely be dealing with a variety of physical and emotional issues.

On a more practical level of amputee marriages they can present several adjustments and difficulties which must be navigated. For couples who have been together for a long time it can be a challenge to adapt to the new lifestyle and expectations which accompany limb loss. Even simple tasks such as getting dressed, toiletry, or going on vacation can require more planning and preparation.

Despite the added challenges, amputee marriages can be incredibly rewarding and fulfilling when both partners are committed to putting the needs of their spouse first. The strength and love of the relationship can be a powerful source of comfort and healing for both parties. Caring for a spouse can be emotionally draining and financially difficult, but it is possible to make a successful marriage despite everything changing. As the quote in the Bible states from Corinthians – Love bears all things, believes all things, hopes all things, endures all things.

For changes to the home, the prerequisite must be to make the home safe and accessible. This can be an expensive task often involving modifications to bathrooms, bedrooms, hallways, and other areas of the house. New furniture such as beds and chairs may also be required to ensure the added comfort and well-being. Additional devices such as stairlifts or ramps may also be necessary to help move around the home. It can be a costly transition. For me personally there have been two things throughout the past fifty years I have needed. One is a stair rail to help going up and down the stairs and secondly a drop-down seat in the shower cubicle to get in and out.

In some cases adapting a car for an amputee may be necessary. This may involve adding special hand controls or seating for a wheelchair. It can also involve reinforcing the frame of the car to make sure it can handle the weight of any prosthetics or wheelchair. Although my first car was a manual car, I had hand controls fitted for the brake and accelerator pedal. Every car after that one has been an automatic without needing any conversion at all. There are many companies who can provide a service unique to the individuals specific requirements, and in the UK, there is funding available for this.

Amputees may need to modify their clothing to accommodate their prosthetics. Adaptions can include taking up hems, adding pockets and modifying materials to have more stretch and ease of movement, These modifications can be quite costly, and they can be time consuming as well. I believe many below knee amputees prefer to wear shorts to make dressing easier. The prostheses, I have found, can wear, or catch on my trousers but it can be different for everyone, as each is unique to the individual.

Caring for an amputee as stated can be difficult and an emotionally draining experience. In some cases it may be necessary for amputee spouses to receive emotional support too. Services such as counselling or therapy are available, but these services can be costly. It can however be invaluable for helping people cope with the stress and emotions associated with their partners disability. If you are a carer then what you do makes a difference, and you must decide what kind of difference you want to make!

Jim - There are significant things to understand regarding the cost of caring and I am going to focus on just one because it is a big one. Namely the roof over your head! I selected this topic because we recently decided to move, and everything is fresh in my mind.

We had lived in the same two-storey house for twenty years prior to my amputation. What was perfectly fine before my amputation, after amputation was no longer tolerable. The doorways were too narrow, the eighteen steps to the second-floor bedrooms were impossible to climb and then difficult for me to navigate even after I had my prosthetic. Using the toilet and shower required difficult maneuvering and adaptive equipment. I slept downstairs in a recliner for three months until my prosthetic was ready. All these adjustments involved additional expense, which included the recliner, grab bars, door ramps, grabbers, walkers, and a wheelchair, as examples. If your amputation is necessary for medical reasons, I would suggest you have a qualified occupational therapist come to your house and evaluate what needs are necessary to adapt your home as much as possible so you will be able to function to the best of your ability. If your amputation was unexpected without having any time to plan, you should still have the home evaluation done while you are in the hospital or rehabilitation hospital. I recommend having as much done as possible before you go home.

Since we have been at our condominium for a while, we had given thought to downsizing even before amputation, but it had become a priority. It was obvious that our existing home was not going to work, and this is where the cost of caring started to significantly ramp up. People tend to forget about the astronomical amount of money we have spent in our lifetime accumulating all the 'stuff' we absolutely had to have and could not live without. Thousands and thousands of dollars' worth of 'stuff' needed selling in garage sales and yard sales for pennies on the dollar if it would even sell at all. We gave what did not sell to a veteran's group thrift store. We gave away about fifty percent of our "must have" possessions with an estimated original value of around fifty thousand dollars. Hard earned money that came out of our pockets over the years evaporated into thin air.

Selling a house can be expensive. Arizona is a rapidly growing state. On average, over one hundred thousand people a year have moved here in the last ten years. At the time we sold the house, it was a sellers' market and our house sold in less than twenty-four hours. Realtors' fees, legal fees, and processing costs, for example, add up quickly and that is a drain on your profit. I realise in parts of this country and other countries there are homes sold at a loss which makes life for an amputee who needs to move because of amputation catastrophic. This creates tremendous pressure on every other aspect of our lives, even to the point of homelessness. It is a fact because of a change of circumstance amputees may lose their homes because of losing their income due to amputation.

Amputation also creates the need for simplification. Make everything as easy and simple as possible because we have a myriad of other issues to deal with. To that end, we decided not to buy a house but to rent an apartment in a fifty-five plus independent living/assisted living, ADA compliant facility. ADA compliance refers to the Americans with Disabilities Act Standards for Accessible Design, which states that all electronic and information technology (like websites) must be accessible to people with disabilities. This meant no more cutting the lawn, cleaning the pool, or painting the walls. Now it is just playing bingo, going to happy hour, and doing chair yoga! All this fun has a price.

We have lived in the condominium for just a couple of years. Our rent has increased by twenty-seven percent during this time and when our lease is due for renewal, it will go up another eight percent! When we came on board, they told us the rents would only increase two to three percent a year. Take heed of renting rule number one, which is landlords tell untruths. The Phoenix area is booming. Thousands of regular apartments are under construction and there are fifteen multi-unit, fifty-five plus complexes under construction. We were able to find a comparable square foot accessible casita (small house or other building) which is thirty-four thousand dollars less annually than where we are living now. Of course, there is the cost of moving which comes into play again. The saga for me continues.

The lesson learned in all this is if you need to move because of your amputation, be sure to do good due diligence!

Chapter 13:

Ageing Impact of Skin

How often do you look into a mirror? Myself is every day because I shave, brush my hair, and clean my teeth. Think about how often you really look though! For me throughout my life it has probably been every three or four years as I have seen the changes slowly happening in hair colour, skin colour and texture.

Ageing can have a significant impact on the skin of amputees, especially on the residual limb. The signs we see in skin ageing are wrinkles, loss of elasticity including loss of volume. For amputees, looking after your skin is so important, moreso around the amputation. The daily impact of wearing a prosthetic, as I do, averaging around sixteen hours a day does take its toll, where any movement is friction, and this can cause excessive wear and tear. I also feel cleanliness is important too because being a hemipelvectomy I am encased in a 'bucket' typed prosthetic, strapped onto me, and heavy sweating occurs every single day particularly in summer. I shower first thing in the morning and last thing at night. To me it is one of life's simple pleasures to take my artificial leg off after a long day and have a hot shower. I liken the feeling of relief to a Victorian lady taking off her corset she has worn all day!

As we age, skin becomes thinner, making it more vulnerable to injury and damage. For amputees who already have skin issues on their residual limb, this can be an area of concern. We can all see how with age the skins natural elasticity reduces with age by a simple pinch test. This loss of elasticity leads to wrinkles and sagging skin. To me there is nothing to compare with the young, and their youthful, vibrant radiance.

Another aspect of ageing is when there is dryness of the skin which tends to produce less oil, making it dry and more prone to cracking. Again this is a challenge for amputees wearing their prosthetic because having dry skin can increase friction and contribute to skin irritation and breakdown as skin is more prone to ageing conditions like eczema, psoriasis, and skin cancer.

As we age our bodies naturally weaken and skin is part of this process. The skin can become more prone to bruising and tearing particularly in areas where there is constant pressure and friction.

If you are fortunate and have good skin and a well fitted prosthetic, life is a much easier, but this is the exception because most suffer from sores or wounds on the pressure and impact points. This is the bane for most of us and the associated pain or infection experienced. If you have a wound and walk on it, then the healing process can be lengthy, and infection becomes a real risk. Of course there will be old and new amputees and there are issues for both. The new amputees need time to harden their skin, and it takes time for this to happen. Initially it is difficult, often painful as the process unfolds and pain barriers are broken, but all this is necessary for the goal of mobility.

For those of us who have used a prosthetic for many years and have 'seasoned' skin, it can still be daunting as age takes its toll. Even though inside I feel as if I am in my mid 30's, outside is more than double that, and it shows! The skin shows some signs of ageing from around twenty five years of age, and not only shows ageing on the surface but it takes place in every layer of the skin.

The first signs of ageing start with fine lines and loss of moisture hence many apply moisturising cream. We all have wrinkles or 'laughter lines' as some call them around the eyes, followed by wrinkles on the forehead. These become more prominent as we get older until they remain, instead of disappearing. It is this which can give the realisation we are ageing, and we are not the invincible person who can steadfastly fight the ageing process.

We all know skin has many layers with the outermost layer of tissue called the epidermal. This layer acts as a repellent and barrier. It keeps moisture in and protects the body against toxins and bacteria. There are many times you read about a wound becoming infected and the impact it can have on the body, even resulting in death in the extreme. These layers of the epidermal and the innermost new skin cells drift towards the surface where they eventually die and shed. In many ways it is good this happens in miniscule detail because if we were able to see everyone's skin being shed, it might look like something out of a horror movie. It would be like seeing the amount of dust particles floating around a room when shafts of sunlight appear.

The skin gradually ages and there is no stopping it, try as we might. As ageing progresses, cell turnover decreases and its ability to retain moisture decreases also resulting in dryer rougher skin. I remember those early days after my amputation when first wearing a prosthesis realising how soft my skin was. It took several months before it hardened to embrace the rigours of friction using the prosthesis.

With my hemipelvectomy amputation the area around the scar line is very taut and always has been. No doubt as I age it has been getting even more taut. What is apparent is this area, about two or three fingers wide of the scar line has always been 'super sensitive'. My view on this matter is the nerve endings below the skin have been exposed and are now much closer to the surface. I cannot stand anyone touching this area because it triggers an immediate pins and needles response as well as a sharp intake of breath from myself for the anticipated pain.

With ageing, the skin becomes less able to self-heal and with a reduced immune system function it is not so efficient at healing any skin infections. Like most amputees you must push yourself at times and there is always the chance of the skin rubbing with the prosthesis as you do this. You learn over time when enough is enough or you suffer the consequences. My take on it is, Walking = Pain = Rubbing = Pain =Wound = Pain. The common factor is pain.

When I was working, my job entailed being involved in huge design and construction projects which meant regularly visiting sites. I remember one in Scotland, and one in Ireland whose construction period were both over a yearlong requiring me to be there all week. I would fly home weekends, on the Friday evening and be off again on the 'red eye' shuttle early Monday morning. There was for me a lot of walking at the airports and often the travelators would not be working, only adding to the exertions. The net result was having a wound that never quite healed due to the walking friction necessary week in, week out. I kept the wound clean, sometimes covering it, but it was a job to ensure no infection started.

When I look on-line at social media Amputee Groups, the most common theme is managing wounds. It is a lifetime quest to understand how best to manage this and what suits you and your skin too. There are so many variables from skin type, amputation height, prosthesis fitting, and amount of walking done, to name a few.

Below the epidermal layers of skin is the middle layer called the dermal layers. This structure consists of collagen, elastin, and connective tissues rich in blood vessels. As we age the collagen levels there slowly decrease as does the elastin. The simple test to show this is to pinch a child's skin to see how quickly it goes back compared to an adult, which goes back slower. This weaker structure makes skin damage easier, leading to reduced circulation. As ageing progresses, the skin is less efficient delivering oxygen and nutrients to the surface. Looking at the beauty of young skin compared to those older is quite apparent especially if you have not cared for your skin, or it has sun damage. Fortunately we are much more aware of the damage done by the sun nowadays than in my early days.

The innermost layers are called the hypodermis layers, which store energy as well as provide the padding and insulation for the body. It also connects the dermis layer to your muscles and bones. As age takes its toll, the lipid storing cells reduce, and sagging commences. I only need to look in a mirror to see the profound effect this has.

I believe it is important to understand the causes and what triggers this effect to try and keep problems at bay. This is of course something we cannot stop because the elixir of life has still to be discovered. Until then we are all ageing as the years drift by. Our biological age, triggers changes in the skin, including cell function which is slowing down over time.

The other aspect is hormonal change where lower levels of oestrogen reduce the signalling capability between cells. This lower blood supply results in lower delivery of nutrients and oxygen to the skins surface.

Genetics play a key role in how skin ages. Thus the skin type we are born with makes a difference to how quickly signs of ageing appear on the skin's surface. Fair skin is more prone to wrinkles than darker skin, likewise uneven skin tone usually means wrinkles appear at a later age. From an amputee's perspective when it comes to the external causes of skin ageing, we focus on the impact to where the amputation is. By doing this we perhaps do not need to focus so much on the sun and pollutants exposure. There are however aspects we can still control somewhat which include nutrients to the body, smoking, and poor skin care.

Without getting into too much depth discussing nutrition it is important to eat lots of antioxidant-rich fruits and vegetables. As much variety as possible should be included, but some foods are known to be particularly high in antioxidants and might even have a skin protecting effect. These include carrots, apricots, orange and yellow fruit and vegetables, blueberries, leafy green vegetables, bell peppers, tomatoes, beans and other pulses, oily fish (such as salmon) and nuts. Whether it is your five or seven a day it is about a balanced diet. These antioxidants neutralise the free radicals which damage skin and speed up the ageing process. The chemicals and nicotine contained in cigarettes also increases the number of free radicals hence the warning to the danger of smoking.

If you can stop smoking it will significantly reduce the number of free radicals which you expose your skin to. As well as improving your skin's appearance, quitting will improve your physical health too. As smokers tell you, it is difficult to give up the drug but I for one have seen the effects of hardening of the arteries on fellow amputees when getting repairs done. It can for some be an insurmountable problem with life threatening consequences.

To an amputee, skin care is important and often there is a price to pay for inappropriate skin care. Skin will age more quickly if it is poorly cared for or if you use products which irritate your skin. Redness or rashes are indicative of such use, or suddenly changing the product you have been using to clean yourself. As your skin changes over time, the way you care for it should also reflect its changing needs. Thorough cleansing, using gentle products appropriate for your skin type, together with the regular inspection will help to care for skin.

Many of the solutions to maintaining or improving your skin can be obvious. Having an active lifestyle is one, but depending on the severity of amputation this can present formidable challenges. For me personally when I walk, the effort expended feels like three or even four times more than someone able-bodied. I also equate walking with pain. We are indeed all different. The other aspect is quality sleep, which allows your body to recover and repair itself.

It is important to understand the type of skin you have. It can be dry, oily, sensitive or a combination of these, or you may just be fortunate and fall into the normal category.

- Dry skin can be itchy, flaky, red, or even feel tight. If you have the extreme of this, then cracking can occur.

- Oily skin looks shiny and can leave a residue when dabbed. With this condition fungal infection can occur.

- Sensitive skin is usually dry and prone to infection.

- Combinations of these conditions on the body can aggravate treatment.

- Normal skin is soft and supple unlike the above conditions.

- The regime for skin care is always personal and not a 'fit all'. An approach sprinkled with some common sense and other care, specific to individual needs, takes time to find suitability. Finding out which products for amputees work best together, how they benefit you, and the right way to use them is a good start. Making sure to rinse away all traces of soap with clean, warm water is important because if it is left on the skin this may cause prosthetic problems later. Many media self-help groups are a good source of information being a common theme discussion point.

Using alcohol-based products on your remaining limb will dry out the skin, leading to cracking or peeling. It also makes sense to apply lotions and moisturizers at night or at another time when you won't be wearing your prosthesis.

Do not shave or use chemical hair remover on your residual limb. When a prosthetic socket rubs against stubble it can cause the hair to grow inward, which can be painful, or lead to infection.

It always amazes me, particularly in the summer how wet the lining of your socket can get from sweating. It is important to clean the socket often to prevent dried perspiration or dirt from accumulating on the inner surface.

Discomfort and skin breakdown are often the first sign that your prosthesis needs an adjustment. It is important to have an interface which fits well. I use a prosthetic sock which I change daily which helps ease the friction occurring when I walk. Even with a good fit, problems can occur as your stump (if you have one) changes in shape and size throughout the day. Weight movement up or down can trigger problems. It is important to add if you have a problem and it persists then it should be discussed with your prosthetist or seek medical advice.

Age-related changes that likely affect skin tolerance for prosthetic use include atrophy and fragility of the dermis thus it is important to maintain your health and lifestyle as best you can. The skin's ability to resist shearing forces is compromised with ageing. Clinically, this is often seen as skin tears, which can easily occur at any interface between the residual limb and the prosthesis. It seems sometimes you just cannot fight the ageing process.

In some ways I consider myself fortunate to not have some of the issues associated with a stump because numerous skin complications can occur around a residual limb. A close eye is needed with regular inspection for early treatment to be given. Skin abrasion or even breakdown is quite common but could be indicative of something else to bring to the attention of your doctor. This may be inadequate sensation which I personally have around the scar line of my amputation. I have always assumed this was the severing of nerves at the time. The downside is you cannot tell what damage you are doing if you cannot feel the area of contact. This inadequate sensation or even blood supply may result in an inability to tolerate the pressure of the prosthesis.

Another aspect is the prosthesis not fitting well. I have experienced many hours in the past just waiting for my leg to be repaired and finally it arrives but is not quite right! Do I say something and wait another long time, or just put up with it and leave. I have seen many accept a leg not quite right because their transport or ambulance is waiting. If they miss this, they must wait more hours for transportation. I would say after many of these experiences, keep on going until you reach something acceptable to you. It will never, ever be 100% but understand what is, and is not acceptable to you, despite other external pressures.

If the prosthesis is worn too long, then blisters can be caused from too much friction. A nylon sock or in my case a cotton sheath worn over the stump will help considerably and more than one may be required. If too many are needed for a degree of comfort, then the prosthesis itself may need to be modified to suite. This why weight uniformity is very important, and for recent amputees it can take many months for the post operation swelling to subside.

Regular inspection is required to treat abrasions and blisters quickly to avoid any serious infections. Cleanliness is next to godliness, and this applies to your residual lower limb. When you are encased for many hours, day in day out, there will always be excessive sweating. Silicone sockets are often a cause for unpleasant odour emanating from it because it will retain moisture, which is often a mixture of sweat and bacteria. Not a nice combination just sitting there hence the need for cleanliness.

It is often recommended to expose the limb to air on a regular basis to help evaporate moisture, but this is on a case by case basis because it is something I have never done or felt needed to be done. The only time I have done this is when the skin is broken quite badly, and the wound needed to heal. This is a rare occurrence for me.

There are numerous skin conditions and the one most found is dermatitis. Dermatitis is a common skin condition that can affect anyone, but amputees are particularly susceptible to this condition. It is characterised by inflammation and irritation of the skin, and it can be caused by a variety of factors including allergies, irritants, and infections. For amputees there are several factors which can contribute to the development of dermatitis, and it is important to understand these factors to prevent and treat this condition.

One of the primary factors that contribute to this in amputees is the use of prosthetic devices. Whilst they provide many benefits, they can also cause skin irritation and inflammation. We have all had this from time to time with the constant friction and pressure of the device against the skin. It can cause damage to the skins protective layer, leading to the development of dermatitis.

Another factor that can contribute to this is the use of skin care products. Many amputees use skin care products to help protect and treat their skin, but some of these products can cause dermatitis. I personally only use E45 which treats dry skin, but products which contain fragrances, preservatives, or other harsh chemicals can irritate the skin and lead to inflammation and itching. Other factors include changes to temperature and humidity, exposure to allergens and irritants, and the presence of other skin conditions such as eczema or psoriasis. Those who have a history of skin sensitivity or who have previously suffered from dermatitis are also at a higher risk of developing this condition.

The symptoms of dermatitis can vary depending on the cause and severity of the condition. Symptoms include redness, itching, burning, stinging, and the development of small bumps or blisters on the skin. In more severe cases, skin may become cracked and bleeding. Treatment for dermatitis typically involves identifying and addressing the underlying cause of the condition. This may involve making changes to the prosthetic device, switching to gentler skin care products, and avoiding exposure to allergens and irritants. In some cases, topical ointments, creams, or oral medication may be prescribed to help manage symptoms and promote healing.

Prevention is also an important aspect which includes regular cleaning and moisturising of the skin, avoiding harsh products and materials, and protecting the skin from temperature extremes and other environmental factors. There are many self-help groups offering advice for all manner of conditions, and it is worth exploring these. Your doctor will also offer various steroid creams, or antihistamines to help too.

There is another condition with a long sounding medical name called verrucous hyperplasia. This is a benign, warty growth which can occur on the skin. While this condition can affect anyone, amputees are particularly susceptible to developing this due to the constant pressure and irritation placed on the skin by their prosthetic device. The exact cause is not fully understood but it is a believed to be related to chronic friction and irritation of the skin. In amputees, friction and irritation can be caused by prosthetic devices which can rub against the skin and cause damage over time. Pressure sores and other skin injuries can also contribute to the development of this.

It is characterised by the development of warty thickened growths on the skin. These groups can be pink, or flesh coloured and may have a rough scaly texture. This typically develops on areas of the skin that are frequently exposed to pressure and friction such as the bottom of the foot or the stump of an amputated limb.

Verrucous hyperplasia is not dangerous, but it can be uncomfortable and unsightly. The growths can also interfere with the proper fit of the prosthesis, making it difficult to wear it comfortably. There are several treatment options available with the most common being to remove the growth using surgery or just freezing them off. In minor cases topical treatments such as salicylic acid or retinoids may be effective in reducing the size and thickness of the growths. I recently saw someone with this when having a repair done at the Enablement Centre. It did look unsightly and was just starting to cause him discomfort at the back of his knee on his residual limb.

Prevention is also an important aspect of managing this and in severe cases it can lead to the development of a type of skin cancer. Amputees who have a history of this or have experienced persistent growths on the skin should be monitored closely by a dermatologist to ensure early detection and treatment of any cancerous growths.

Our skin is the organ which meets with the rest of the world. As the body's largest organ, skin protects against germs, regulates body temperature, and enables tactile sensations. It holds body fluids in, preventing dehydration, and keeps harmful microbes out, without which we would get infections.

Our skin is full of nerve endings that help you feel things like heat, cold, and pain.

Your skin makes up about 15% of your total body weight. The average adult has almost twenty-one square feet of skin that contains over eleven miles of blood vessels. A single square inch of skin has about three hundred sweat glands, which explains why we sweat so. The thickest skin is on your feet and the thinnest area of skin is on your eyelids. It is fundamental to our existence, so ask yourself the question, 'Why would you not want to look after it and keep it as healthy as you can?'".

Jim – I am the poster child for this chapter because our skin is the "Canary in the coal mine", or your early warning system. As we get older, everything in our bodies deteriorates including our skin. Skin issues were a significant contributor to my amputation. I have been a diabetic for over thirty years, maybe longer, and developed diabetic ulcers on my lower legs which required professional wound care treatment eventually leading to amputation of my lower right leg. Approximately eighty six thousand people in the United States undergo limb loss directly related to diabetes annually. Many skin issues are directly caused by diabetes which is directly related to causing most lower-extremity amputations. It is the "Vicious triangle", where skin infections can go uncontrolled and cause the limb to be infected resulting in amputation.

The number one cause of amputations, especially lower limb amputations, are vascular diseases which includes diabetes and peripheral arterial disease. Estimates range from 54% up to 80% in some studies. Other studies show up to 55% of people with diabetes who already have a lower extremity amputation will require amputation of the second leg within two to five years.

Changes in blood sugar levels can leave the skin more susceptible to infections. These infections may take longer to heal and lead to severe complications. The American Diabetes Association lists several types of infections which can occur. Skin conditions caused by diabetes typically involve either bacterial or fungal infection and are therefore at high risk for infections. My advice if you are diabetic and an amputee, or contemplating amputation, is to do everything possible to manage and control your diabetes. If you are not diabetic, do everything you can to not join the club.

Diabetes is a "silent killer" and remains a major health crisis causing a significant rise in lower limb amputations in America, despite medical advances and prevention efforts. The prevalence of diabetes (type 2 diabetes and type 1 diabetes) will increase by 54% to nearly fifty five million Americans between 2015 and 2030. Annual deaths attributed to diabetes will climb by 38% to just under four hundred thousand and the total annual medical and societal costs related to diabetes will increase 53% to more than $622 billion by 2030.

Chapter 14:

Arthritis

Many people suffer from arthritis, and it can be debilitating for amputees because it causes stiffness, swelling and pain in joints. Millions of people around the world suffer from this and age is no discriminator. I remember many years ago when I was attending a local polytechnic doing a course there. A young guy who was there, like me in his early twenties, had arthritis very badly. In two years, his walking became shuffling, and his deterioration together with the associated pain he was in was awful to see.

It mostly starts among people between the ages of forty and sixty and is more common in women than men. There are now drugs that can slow down an over-active immune system and therefore reduce the pain and swelling in joints. In America one in four have arthritis and although common in older adults, 50% have it over sixty five.

There are many forms of arthritis but the two most common are osteoarthritis and rheumatoid arthritis. Osteoarthritis is the most common and often develops in people in their mid-forties, which incidentally was my age when it was diagnosed in my knee. Osteoarthritis initially affects the smooth cartilage lining of the joint. This makes movement more difficult than usual, leading to pain and stiffness. It usually affects the knees, hips, spine, and hands because once the cartilage lining starts to roughen and thin out, the tendons and ligaments must work harder.

I have heard from several people who have broken their arm or leg early in life and because of the injury, it brings arthritis later in life. You often see the effects of impact sports, such a football or rugby, to see ageing ex-players somewhat struggling with their mobility. It is the loss of cartilage which can lead to bone rubbing on bone, altering the shape of the joint and forcing the bones out of their normal position. For me only having the one knee, the pain was at times excruciating but a simple scrape operation using micro-surgery helped this a lot.

Rheumatoid arthritis is less common than osteoarthritis and often starts when a person is between thirty and fifty years old, with women more likely to be affected than men. In rheumatoid arthritis, the body's immune system targets affected joints, which leads to pain and swelling. The outer covering of the joint is the first place affected which can then spread across the joint, leading to further swelling and a change in the joint's shape. This may cause the bone and cartilage to break down. People with rheumatoid arthritis can also develop problems with other tissues and organs in their body.

It is important to understand the physical effects of arthritis on an amputee, They often experience extreme mobility restrictions due to the degenerative effects on the surrounding joint structures. This can lead to difficulties in performing even the basic activities of daily living such as standing, walking, and using the hands. An example of this for me is using my hand when pushing up from a chair to stand. At times the pain in my hands hurts considerably and sometimes it is easier to push with my palms of my hand flat. We are all constantly adjusting to the ageing process whether we realise it or not.

The mental effects of arthritis on amputees can also be severe due to the physical limitations imposed by their disabilities. They may suffer from feelings of loneliness, isolation, and depression and may also feel unable to participate in activities they once enjoyed, leading to a decrease in self-esteem. The physical and mental effects of arthritis are numerous with social, economic, and cultural implications as many of these individuals may not have the same access to necessary healthcare or other services as those without disabilities. On the bright side advances in medical technology have allowed more precise and effective treatments although the effects are far reaching.

Joint pain may lead to an increase in the risk of falling, reducing the quality of life, and increasing the risk of hospitalisation. In addition it may also lead to changes in the skin, muscles, and bones of the amputated area resulting in more frequent infections and more difficulty in finding comfortable prosthetics.

There is an increased load on the non-amputated leg of long-term prosthetic users which can lead to an increased risk of developing osteoarthritis. They obviously experience larger forces at the knee of their non-amputated limb than people without lower extremity amputations. There is also a connection between post-amputation weight gain and arthritis whereby inactivity weakens the muscles and bones and thereby increases stress on the knee joint. Just simple regular walking for those high functioning amputees subjects the joints to added stress on their intact limbs.

A survey of male war veterans with unilateral major lower limb amputations developed significantly more osteoarthritis of the hip than expected on both sides. Amputation was also associated with loss of bone density. It was also noted above-knee amputees developed significantly more hip osteoarthritis and reduced bone tissue density of greater severity in the amputated side than below-knee amputees.

Among elderly amputees a number also have a condition where arteries are narrowing which can give rise to numerous heart conditions and Parkinson's disease. All of this can add to the recovery after amputation and delay progress.

For an Amputation above the knee joint it means control of the prosthesis is much more difficult with the energy expenditure at least 50% more than normal walking. I do believe for those like me, being a hemipelvectomy, the energy expenditure is far higher than 50%. For those who have bilateral amputations this causes even more difficulty. All of this is compounded by arthritis in the joints of the remaining lower limb and in the hinge joints of the amputated limb which are likely to be painful and stiff with a limited range of movement, possible deformity, and weak muscles.

Weight bearing and attempts to walk impose stresses which frequently seem to start a flare-up in disease activity. Similar problems in the joints of hands, arms and shoulders make it difficult to hold walking aids, pull the prosthesis on and off and in manipulating the buckles, straps and belts which secure the prosthesis. I have started to struggle moreso just putting shoes on as my joints in my hands become more painful and I am unable to bend them as before. By wearing a prosthesis it means weight is distributed between two legs and this reduces the stress on the residual leg and upper limbs. I am normally more comfortable wearing my prosthesis than without, and certainly sitting in a chair.

If as an ageing amputee you wear your prosthesis then you can transfer without help from bed to chair, and from chair to toilet, but not otherwise. Wearing the prosthesis therefore maintains a degree of independence. The level of mobility achieved by lower limb amputees with arthritis is poor, and they are likely to be chairbound, although it is worthwhile supplying a prosthesis as they make transfers feasible and enhance their independence and quality of life.

There have even been cases where elderly patients with rheumatoid arthritis have undergone amputation because of necrotising fasciitis, which is a rare bacterial infection which spreads quickly and can cause death. In such cases they have regained the ability to walk with a prosthetic limb.

We are all different and what suits one does not for another. I know if I do not wear my prosthesis when sitting in a chair, after a few minutes I get back ache because I am unable to sit normally in a level plain, due to the type of amputation I have had.

One of the downsides of having an amputation is about the entailed reduced mobility experienced for several months. It is easy to comfort eat or keep the food intake the same as when you were mobile, which is then not burnt off through exercise. This results in weight increase and is a common occurrence. Weight uniformity is most important for amputees and cannot be overemphasised. The type of food being eaten should also be considered to maintain a healthy body not prone to arthritis. A good balanced diet is right for everyone.

Processed fast food like breakfast cereal, and baked goods are typically high in refined grains, added sugar, preservatives, and other potentially inflammatory ingredients, all of which may worsen arthritis symptoms. This is why it is important to consider what you are eating and how best to help the arthritis from flaring or worsening. Dietary fats can certainly influence inflammation which is a major factor in rheumatoid arthritis.

The risks and consequences of not making dietary changes include increased inflammation and greater risks of other health issues. The benefits of making positive changes to an amputee's diet, such as reducing the risk of further joint damage and improving mobility will give both short and long term benefit. An amputee living with arthritis should include such foods which reduce inflammation and promote joint health. When it comes to making lasting dietary changes, the overall impact will be positive because a healthy diet can have a positive impact on the quality of life.

To complement an improved eating diet to help with arthritis it is worth considering taking joint supplements. Glucosamine and chondroitin have decades of clinical studies and research behind them to prove they help millions of people cope with hip, joint and muscle problems. Other supplements like turmeric, hyaluronic acid and MSM (Methylsulfonylmethane) are beneficial with each offering support in treating arthritis.

Looking at each supplement: -

Glucosamine – helps reduce inflammation and stiffness which in turn reduces osteoarthritis pain.

Chondroitin – reduces joint stiffness.

Turmeric – provides support for joints and reduces grinding, improves flexibility reduces discomfort.

MSM – has anti-inflammatory and antioxidants effects.

Hyaluronic Acid - a natural substance found in the fluids in the eyes and joints and acts as a cushion and lubricant in the joints and other tissues.

All the above, or a combination of them have proven health benefits and help promote the bodies long term health by boosting the body's defence against arthritis. In the body we have cartilage which is produced naturally but when it wears out over time it can result in grinding bones and other issues causing pain and difficulty in mobility. This degradation of cartilage can be slowed down by taking supplements aiding joint health.

Amputees may face a variety of joint health issues due to their limb loss. Joint pain, contractures, and limited mobility are common issues faced due to changes in the body's alignment. Other issues such as scars, skin irritation, and phantom limb pain can also affect joint health. Good health joints can reduce the risk of further injury, improve the ability to perform daily activities, and increase confidence and self-esteem. Good health joints certainly help to avoid the effects of arthritis.

Joint health by having regular physical therapy can help maintain physical fitness and strength, in addition using specialised orthotic devices which help provide support for the joint can also reduce the risk of further injury. It is also important to keep your joints flexible and mobile by regular stretching and doing a range of motion exercises.

Being an amputee makes you strong, our pain levels we live with rise, and remember what does not kill you makes you stronger. We do not know how strong we really are until being strong is the only choice. Nobody can take away your pain, but do not let pain take away your happiness.

Jim - It has taken fourteen chapters of this book for me to realize that every subject John has covered so far, has been talking about me!

Nearly 50% of all adults who are sixty five or older have arthritis. When you add the disability factor, the numbers get even larger. Amputees are at higher risk for arthritic issues because of the added stress we put on our bodies as well as other health issues like diabetes. We have already established the relationship between diabetes and lower limb amputations. Severe joint pain is more common among the general population with arthritis who also have other chronic conditions including diabetes (40.9%), and among adults with a physical disability (45.6%). Statistically, when the age factor is included, more than half of us will have some form of severe arthritis pain as compared to the general population.

Falling is a major issue for us ageing amputees. Arthritis and ageing compound the problem. Comparing adults aged forty five years and older who do not have arthritis to adults forty five years and over with arthritis, we are four times more likely to have two or more falls and five times more likely to have a fall injury. People with a lower limb amputation in the first four years of amputation or with four or more health-related problems like arthritis are at an increased risk. So, watch your step!

I have been luckier than most because the amount of arthritis I have is minimal compared to what others report as having. Sixty five years ago, I dislocated my right shoulder while playing high school football and it required surgical repair. The procedure at that time was done with a chainsaw and crowbar compared to today's sophisticated methods. Physical therapy was unheard of. They kept my arm immobile and strapped to my chest for six weeks. Today they have you moving within hours after surgery. Despite all that, it has held up very well, up until about a year ago. It is now a bone-on-bone situation. Since I need to use a walker due to balance issues, it has put increased pressure on my shoulders and has sped up the deterioration process significantly. I have had four major back surgeries to correct arthritic pain and they have been successful as have been two knee replacements. Luckly, I have not had any arthritic issues with my hips.

I am considering getting pain management shots for my shoulders soon. Regarding pain management, I am astonished at the rapid growth of the pain management segment of medical care. It seems like a significant number of physicians are moving into that business. Every week a new pain management cure or procedure appears on TV guaranteed to make your pain disappear! I wish it were true.

There are more than one hundred types of arthritis and for many (or most) of them there is no compelling evidence that individual foods play a significant role in disease development, symptoms, or disease severity. There are connections between diet and arthritis worth noting. Some people notice certain foods seem to make joint pain or arthritis worse. In such cases, it is reasonable to avoid those foods. However, a highly restrictive diet is not generally necessary for people with common types of arthritis. There is some evidence that an "anti-inflammatory" diet, such as the Mediterranean diet, may be helpful in reducing body-wide inflammation and joint pain in certain types of arthritis, such as rheumatoid arthritis. Based on this information, I think it is fair to say most of us are dealing with some form of arthritis or will be. Like many of the other challenging aspects of life as an ageing amputee, we deal with it as best we and our medical support groups can.

Chapter 15:

Weight Control

We seem to be bombarded nowadays from every media outlet about dieting and so-called new fad dieting methods. It goes without saying Being an amputee for most, means having to re-appraise what living an active life can entail. If the many years of being an amputee has taught me anything it has been to work as hard as I can and maintain my weight as much as I possibly can.

Amputation is not a static disability, but a progressive deteriorating condition which affects the health status of amputees over time. This is why, as ageing happens it is important to not be too hard on yourself when you find the rigours of exercise taking their toll on you. The saying. 'Everything in moderation', springs to mind.

Those with lower limb amputations will naturally have reduced levels of activity and any weight movement up or down, if too much, will affect the wearing of a prosthesis. I know mine feels a little different if I have put a few pounds on, and I cut back on food for a few days to get a more comfortable feeling. I always think the prostheses will not change, only my body can, and to me there is only the one variable. If I needed to get the prostheses altered, it for me is a much more difficult path to go down with added discomfort, when compared to less intake of food. I have spent so many hours of my life getting my prosthesis repaired or made I do not want to make further visits self-induced.

Exercising can come in many forms. I have a friend of mine who is close to my age and exercises every day in the gym. I also know someone who is less mobile and does exercise just sitting down in the chair, whereas mine often comes in the form of gardening. Do whatever suits you but do remember a healthy body will prepare and assist your overall well-being, mentally, physically, and emotionally.

If your weight gain or loss is significant then the prosthesis needs to be safe to carry you. Safety is paramount and you need 100% confidence for every step you make. It takes time to build this confidence into your psyche. Your fluid balance in the body can also affect your stump size. Often kidney and heart conditions can cause an imbalance, and it is important to understand the underlying cause of weight movement. There may need to be dialogue with both the doctor and your prosthetist.

Water retention known as oedema is caused by a build-up of fluid in your body's tissue and can be seen in feet, ankles, and legs as well as hands, face, and abdomen. There are numerous reasons for this occurring such as sitting in one position for too long, which many amputees can relate to. The cause list for this occurring is quite long and includes certain drugs for blood pressure, anti-inflammatory, steroids, and anti-depressants, to name a few. It can also be indicative of a more serious health condition around liver, kidney, or heart disease.

To help improve this, salt reduction or exclusion of it may be recommended. Too much salt upsets the sodium balance in your bloodstream and as it tries to dilute the salt, by retaining water, bloating occurs. It is important to understand what you eat, for instance processed and packaged food are often high in salt content if you read the narrative on the packaging. It is amazing how finely balanced our bodies are and we are all guilty of taking this for granted. We all know fresh and whole foods are good for us and contain salt, electrolytes, potassium, and magnesium which are essential to maintain the fluid balance in your body.

Drinking plenty of water helps flush out excess salt and water retention. No matter what you do it will always be good to maintain a balanced diet. Every generation seems to race around faster and faster and have less time for food preparation. Pre-packed food is far more common nowadays than in mine, being a post-war child. Plenty of fruit like avocados, melons, bananas, and citrus fruits all play their part, along with nuts and herbs. I remember when I was young and the Christmas stocking was hung up, Santa always left an orange in it. What luxury that was. It is never too late to change your mindset around your food routine, even if you have a serious condition. 'Every little help's', as they say!

Not everyone has access to a gym or facilities close by and it is worth contacting local fitness centres or healthcare facilities before any training sessions are planned. The staff there will be trained in all aspects of health care and will discuss any barriers or challenges likely to be encountered. Where the building is, from an accessibility point of view, can be important as some facilities are upstairs, which can be a problem. Is there parking nearby, can you access easily with your prosthesis on, using crutches or a wheelchair and are toilets accessible? Sometimes these facilities have personal trainers, and a specific fitness regime and program can be instigated to personally suit you.

In summary, managing weight control for amputees can be challenging but the key areas to concentrate on are: -

- Adopt a healthy diet: Eating a well-balanced diet is crucial for maintaining a healthy weight. Include a variety of foods such as lean protein, whole grains, fruits, and vegetables. Avoid processed foods and sugar laden drinks.

- Engage in physical activity: Physical activity is essential for losing weight and maintaining a healthy weight. Find activities that feel comfortable, such as swimming, cycling, or wheelchair sports. You can also work with the physical therapist to develop an exercise plan that suits your needs.

- Consider prosthetics: You may or may not have a prosthesis, but legs and arms can help amputees in many instances become more active, which can promote weight management. Consult with a prosthetist to ensure you have the proper prosthetics to meet your needs.

- Monitor caloric intake: To manage weight it is essential to monitor your calorie intake. Use a food diary or calorie tracking app to stay on top of your daily intake.

- Seek professional guidance. Consider working with a registered dietitian or a weight management specialist to develop a personalised plan for managing your weight. They can help you set realistic goals and provide ongoing support.

From an amputee perspective, and of course a health one, the yo-yo effect of dieting is certainly one to avoid. Maintaining a uniform weight is important because of the prosthesis. If you change shape, the prosthesis does not, and this means discomfort through sores and even cuts. After amputation it is understandably a period of inactivity. This may include pre-operation, in which case a period of immobilisation through ill-health, perhaps leading to amputation, is a cause for not following a careful review of your weight management. It may be the last thing on your mind at the time where any mobility is hindered, especially in a life threatening situation.

The other aspect of managing weight is to avoid comfort eating. This is eating or overeating to relieve stress, anxiety, or boredom, all of which can be symptomatic of having an amputation. There are other reasons like sadness (at losing a limb), anger, fear, resentment even shame. There are and always will be reasons to do this, but it must be a mind-set change to avoid the slippery slope and downstream problems. In these times it can be difficult looking just a day or two ahead let alone weeks or months, but the medical and family support network need to be mindful of this.

With my high amputation, I sit in a 'bucket type' socket which has a hip lock. When seated at a table for eating and I lean over, the socket is at an angle of around eighty five degrees to my horizontal thigh on my prosthesis. This means when I lean over the table to eat from my plate I can only lean so far, and the rim of the socket digs into my stomach. There have been times when on a new leg, this angle has been closer to ninety degrees, and it becomes quite difficult to eat, and a major change is needed.

If my weight has increased only by a few pounds, as I eat, I can feel the discomfort because my stomach rides on the socket and belt around my waist. I then need to ease off the food intake to reduce this to a comfortably, acceptable weight. This normally entails cutting back significantly for a week or two. It is like an alarm clock to me, which if I ignore would lead to a major change in socket design and all the hassle of getting it done. The same effect occurs on a residual leg socket if weight movement is too great, but not quite as drastic to affect the way you lean over to eat.

When eating in response to emotions it is called emotional eating and we all do it occasionally. Eating lights up the reward system in your brain and makes you feel better, but doing this on a continual basis needs to be addressed. We all need food and is part of celebrations and the connection is there from an early age. Eating food releases dopamine which is a brain chemical making you feel good. The aim is to allow yourself to make a conscious decision about when, what, and how you eat. It is not a disorder but can lead to an eating disorder.

We all have a routine when it comes to our eating habits and there are a few signs to look out for. If for instance when you feel stressed, you eat food, this could be an indicator of a not so good habit. Likewise eating when you are not hungry, which may take the form of sweets, cakes, or chocolate is only acceptable in moderation.

The more you understand and recognise your own eating habits and what your feelings are at the time, then it can be the first steps to introduce change for a healthier lifestyle. Even recording in a diary when you eat, but are not hungry, is a first step to see patterns or triggers starting. In this way recording what was happening and your feelings at the time may capture something you recognise in your emotions wanting you to eat.

We are fortunate to live in a 'land of plenty' and to live a comfortable life compared to some Third World Countries, and where the next meal comes from is not known. To really understand the physical signs of hunger and your own experience of feeling them, the following signs are indicative of them. Stomach grumbling, low energy levels, difficulty focusing, mood swings, shaky and increased thought of food.

A lot of people have been on and off diets for so long it is a way of life. It can be hard to understand the prompts your body gives you for both being full and hungry. If you can understand when you are physically hungry then it can help you know when you are eating for emotional reasons. One other point worth exploring is the way our lives are dictated by time. We might have breakfast around 7.00, lunch around 13.00, and a dinner at 18.00, give or take an hour or so. We have a mindset to eat then. In the distant past without watches or clocks we were more governed by instinct and ate when hungry. Sometimes if I am still full-up from the previous night's dinner I may not have breakfast until 10.00, and then may only need an evening meal having skipped lunch. We do need to listen much more to our bodies and not clock watch for food. People need to understand the difference between want and need.

Being an amputee compounds issues around weight control but healthcare or mental health professionals, or even a dietician will help to address both the physical and mental sides of emotional eating. Remember dieting is the only game where you win when you lose!

Jim - *I have gained and lost three people in my lifetime! I have been up and down more times than a wooden horse on a carousel. I have spent enough money to put my kids through Harvard on diet plans, food plans, pills, potions and lotions, nutritionists, gym memberships, hypnotism, and every other scheme imaginable. That pretty much describes my lifetime battle with weight control. It would be hypocritical of me to stand here on one leg and try to relay how important weight control is to prevent diabetes and subsequently an amputation. We all know it. It is just harder for some of us than others to make it happen. As we get older it becomes even harder in my opinion*

I must say however, I have really worked hard at trying to control my weight and practice good blood sugar management since my amputation. My A1C levels (haemoglobin and blood sugar levels) are very acceptable. I fear becoming one of the statistics I mentioned earlier which is, 'Other studies show up to 55% of people with diabetes who already have a lower extremity amputation will require amputation of the second leg within two to five years.' I have just beaten the five-year mark, however, two of the three arteries in my remaining lower leg are completely blocked and the third artery is partially blocked but thanks to my fantastic vascular doctor inserting some stints, it is functioning at 70% capacity. From time to time, I will have an outbreak of diabetic ulcers on my lower leg which require professional wound care attention along with antibiotics. I have currently been receiving treatment from home health nurses who specialize in wound care. Diabetic ulcers heal very slowly.

While this chapter focuses on weight control, I am endeavouring to show the direct connection between weight control and problems which result from obesity like diabetes and subsequent high probability of amputation. Obesity contributes to up to half of new diabetes cases annually in the United States and is a major risk factor for developing type 2 diabetes. More than 90% of type 2 diabetics are overweight or obese. Obesity is linked to between 30-53% of new diabetes cases in the U.S. yearly. Obesity-related diabetes varies by gender and race/ethnicity, and the greatest impact is among non-Hispanic white females. Overweight and obesity account for 44% of the diabetes cases worldwide. Women with a body mass index (BMI) of 30 kg/m2 have a twenty eight times greater risk of developing diabetes than do women of normal weight. Food for thought!

Chapter 16:

Ageing of the Body

Life invariably gives you a second chance, it is called today, not tomorrow, which at sixteen it did. Being now in the 'Autumn' years of my life I do contemplate what happens when I die and know then, I will not have to wear a prosthesis! It is after all a positive way to look at my own mortality.

We all think about our mortality and not only what happens after death but the way we die and leave this earthly presence. The ravages of time take their toll on the body especially if you lose a limb along life's journey, or if you were born without one, or more. Whatever limb you lose, if you wear a prosthesis, be it an arm or a leg then it is not a natural appendage to your body. Not being natural, and with our hunter gatherers body having evolved over hundreds of thousands of years, this knew attachment to your body, although helping, does cause some amount of misalignment. This misalignment can cause some minor discomfort right through to major pain at every step or movement made. The long term effect of this is an individually unique issue which might be minor, right through to scoliosis of the spine or more severe.

When the impact of wearing something which is unnatural in your body for years and years happens, your own genes can play an important part in the outcome or progression of the effect. For instance if you have been blessed with a strong bone structure through ancestral legacy this must help ease the burden rather than if you have a hereditary weaker structure. My wife laughs at my hypothesis that for several previous generations my ancestors were bricklayers and stone masons. I suggested to her my genes had therefore given me a stronger structure moreso than others, which is just as well given the size and shape of my artificial leg I must wear.

I remember in my twenties and thirties feeling blessed with how strong I felt and having a good healthy body, less one limb. In my forties the first signs of wear and tear appeared with my knee, which was obviously to be expected with the additional work it must do. Having it scraped helped, and the occasional ibuprofen to alleviate the swelling at times worked for me.

It was around this time in my forties I needed to re-educate myself with how I should proceed from this point onwards. I found stairs at times more difficult, especially on my knee, and at that time in my life I made the conscious decision to use a lift whenever I could, rather than stairs.

I can recall an incident in my early thirties when I was at work and needed to go up from floor level three to floor level five and decided to catch a lift. When it arrived it was full, and I squeezed in. The guy nearest the lift button asked me which floor I wanted, and I told him. With it being only two floors up he made the caustic remark, 'do you have an artificial leg then', to which I replied, 'I do actually.' There was complete silence in the lift, and he was so embarrassed by his thoughtless throwaway comment as I walked out because he could see for himself, I was disabled. I trust he learned a lesson.

By using a lift and not stairs where I can, has for me, had a positive impact on the progressive wear and tear of my knee which has over the years proved to be manageable. In hindsight perhaps I should have always done it, but sometimes waiting around for ages until the lift finally arrives used to test my patience, particularly when work priorities were my focus of attention.

The impact of ageing is so wide-ranging and such a complex area to be specific because there is no one-size-fits-all answer. In general, amputees experience a range of age-related health issues such as increased risks for arthritis and reduced muscle strength. Unlike most people, who naturally age and experience the decline in physical strength and flexibility, amputees often experience an accelerated decline in their remaining limb and bodily functions. This makes living with an amputation much more difficult than ageing normally. It is not something I have thought about too much over the years, but as you age there is a realisation of everyday things becoming more difficult. I have always tried to embrace the ageing process as being something natural to everyone who has been born. To me ageing is an acceptance of living and part of the cycle we are all on.

When it comes to physical health, where the declining physical stamina and strength experienced is apparent, they may also suffer from more frequent aches and pains due to their prosthetic. This can result in sores from rubbing the skin when walking, or just sitting still too long. I know for me if I sit down for too long, I often suffer from phantom pains then, or the next day.

The amputation itself may cause changes in the remaining body such as reduced grip strength in the opposite arm or hand as well as changes in the remaining leg if the amputation was present on one foot or leg. For me when I walk, I use my right hand to grip a catch on my prosthesis to help me when walking. Unfortunately I am experiencing some pain in both hands with arthritis and at times this is proving difficult for me when walking. I am fortunate to still be able to walk a little though, and I am grateful for that. Again all of this is unique to the individual.

Amputees may also experience psychological and emotional changes with ageing. The amputation itself can make them feel isolated from the rest of society as well as make it feel like their body is no longer their own. This may result in anxiety, depression, and feel a lack of control in their lives. All this can make it difficult to adjust to their new body if it is a recent loss as well as to prevent them from fully embracing their life after amputation.

In addition to physical and psychological changes they may also have to adjust to changes in their social lives. It may be difficult for amputees to find employment due to their physical limitations as well as to build relationships with people who do not understand their amputation and the impact to their life. Finding friends in the support system can be difficult since many people are not comfortable adjusting or discussing their disability. This is found moreso with some of the older stoic generation who then disconnect with people around them leading to feelings of loneliness and isolation and further complicating the emotional process of ageing.

This somewhat unique process of ageing differs drastically from normal ageing. Not only will amputees experience some of the same physical and psychological changes, but they will also experience unique changes that no one else is able to truly understand. It is important to understand these changes and recognise the difficulties being faced as they age to better support those living with an amputation. I have met many amputees over the years and some you know are strong and courageous, and as bad as it is, still embrace their newly found or imposed disability. Unfortunately there are many others who you can see are struggling and have a negative mind-set. These will not, or are unable to, accept what has happened and the need to make major changes in their lives.

The physical impact of ageing on the body and a decrease in strength, balance and mobility can make walking and standing much more difficult. This can lead to a decrease in physical activity which in turn leads to an overall decrease in circulation and an increase in fatigued muscles and joints. In becoming weakened it may lead to an increased risk of injury or falls, chronic pain and swelling. It is a knock-on effect from one thing to another.

There are a few things which can be done to make the ageing process easier for amputees. One of the most important is to encourage them to remain physically active. This can help to improve circulation, alleviate fatigue as well as maintaining strength and mobility in the remaining limbs. It should not be underestimated how important it is to provide emotional support thus creating a safe and secure space to discuss their disability and the difficulties associated with it.

Another aspect of ageing is to understand chronic pain and swelling which is a common occurrence particularly if the person suffers from other health complaints. In simple terms chronic pain is defined as pain that lasts longer than twelve weeks and is not caused by physical injury or illness. Swelling occurs when extra fluid collects in the body, which in turn can cause discomfort, inflammation, and pain. Ageing amputees are more likely to experience chronic pain and swelling than those who are not amputees. This is due to a variety of factors such as the loss of protective structures and sensory nerve endings in the amputation area. Additionally the use of prosthetic devices can cause friction and additional stress on the affected area, leading to further pain and swelling.

Education on treatments and medication include sterile and anti-inflammatory drugs, which include opioids, and are key to managing chronic pain and swelling. The importance of physical therapy such as a range of motion exercises and aquatic therapy should not be underestimated in keeping healthy. I have always enjoyed swimming because there is no pain involved in moving around in water and it is a wonderful feeling being tired without the associated pain I would have experienced through walking.

Additionally guidelines on choosing and caring for prosthetics should be provided or discussed with the prosthetist and physiotherapist to ensure the appropriateness of a prosthesis. Discussing lifestyle modifications such as reducing the amount of stress, improving diet and exercise all help, including maintaining proper posture. This ensures alignment of purpose, well-being, medication, and treatment. As stated, the importance of proper nutrition, appropriate exercise, and proper care of the prosthetic can reduce the risk of developing chronic pain and swelling.

Prosthetic technology may not always be able to keep up with the physical demands of older amputees, leading to a lack of independence and mobility. I know after using a similar prosthetic leg for over fifty years I would be reluctant to change unless there were significant advantages to be had, especially as my walking in years to come will be limited. Furthermore an ageing amputee's community and living situation may impede their ability to receive care from trained professionals. All these factors can affect a person's mental and physical health, leading to feelings of isolation and depression. It can be quite daunting depending on the individual being able to cope with so much change happening in a short period of time.

It is important that ageing amputees receive adequate care and support to maximise their quality of life. Physical therapies and medication should be tailored to the individuals' specific needs. Healthcare providers and carers must work together to ensure the individual is getting the care they need and to ensure a comfortable and safe lifestyle. This can be done through patient advocacy groups, support systems, media groups and other community resources. By staying informed and advocating for themselves, ageing amputees can manage their condition more effectively and lead healthier lives.

We are all ageing, and the legacy, or gift of life, is death. We all think about death from time to time, and I have, when facing life or death at only sixteen, and later too when you pass your three score and ten years. What helps me to not be too anxious about what the future may hold is the thought that billions of people before me have faced the same thoughts, and it is only natural to contemplate your demise from time to time. One thing I remember reading was. 'Life is not measured by the number of breaths we take, but by the moments that take our breath away.' Make sure you have some of those moments.

Jim - We progress, or maybe it should be called regress, through life. The day we are born is the pinnacle of our lives. Every day after that is one day closer to the final day of the ageing process. While this chapter deals primarily with our ageing bodies, there are other ageing processes we go through, and they are all tied together and are interrelated to each other to make up who we are. They include emotional, mental, psychological, neurological, spiritual, intellectual as well as our physically ageing bodies. If you want some humour, take a "Selfie, "and, if you still have it, go dig out your High School Yearbook and look up your senior picture and compare them! Who ever thought you would look like that?

As amputees, I believe we physically age a little faster especially lower limb amputees because I think I did. Studies have revealed that crutch walking and prosthetic ambulation require the same energy expenditure. There is no significant difference between the energy requirements of ambulating with knee locked or unlocked and that sixty five percent more energy is required at approximately one-half the normal speed of ambulation for above-knee amputees as compared to normal persons. The numbers are a little lower for below-knee amputees. The rule of thumb is the shorter the residual limb, the more energy is required to function. The conclusion is to do as much physical exercise as you possibly can to get in the best shape to be able to function as normally as you can.

While I had a fair amount of physical therapy after my amputation, no one fully explained the reasoning and importance of continuing to exercise on an ongoing basis to compensate for the extra energy needed to function reasonably well. I mistakenly thought that once I had a prosthetic, I would be able to walk like a 'Normal person'. This is a common misconception for new amputees. There is also additional stress and pressure put on other parts of our bodies. For instance I must use a walker due to balance issues. I personally have experienced accelerated wear and tear on my shoulders and elbows as well as my back and artificial knee on my "good leg".

One day you are fine, the next day you are missing a part of your body. Automatically, all the other ageing processes mentioned above kick into high gear. I call them, "The ageing bundle" because you are now needing to deal with issues that were not present yesterday. Simple things you did without thinking now require you to figure out how to accomplish them; like getting the box of cereal from the top shelf or getting a good fitting prosthetic. Little by little these thousands of 'ageing bundle' issues begin to wear us down, accelerating the ageing process. There is then the icing on the cake, namely phantom pains which makes the stress factors go through the roof adding wrinkles on your face and a giant jump forward toward the final day of the ageing process.

My solution is to use my brain and focus on positives. Positive thoughts and positive actions. I focus on getting out of my mental shell and discomfort zone and focus on helping others. When you are focused on others, you do not have time to wallow in your own pool of issues. I know it sounds corny and simplistic, but it works for me.

Chapter 17:

Amputee Falls

I have never met an amputee who has not fallen over. There are two issues when falling. One is how you fall, and any damage caused, and the second is getting up again. Henry Ford said, 'The greatest glory in living lies not in never falling, but in rising every time we fall.'. I do believe the analogy could apply to amputees!

Amputees face a unique set of challenges in their daily lives which include difficulty with mobility, balance, and stability. One of the most significant challenges is the risk of falling which can lead to serious injuries, loss of independence, and even death in the extreme. The problem associated with falling is a complex issue which is somewhat unique to the person. For instance if I fall backwards, I do try to not bang my head too hard, but the prosthesis takes me where I fall as I have virtually no control over how I fall because it is attached around my waist. Likewise if I fall forward then I never know where or how I am going to fall. All I can do is use my arms to try and avoid too much damage. On average I fall around two or three times a year, whereas others are moreso because of other factors. Just remember, what defines us is how we rise after falling.

The factors that contribute to the risk of falling are numerous and varied. One of the most significant factors is a loss of sensation in the residual limb which occurs after amputation surgery. Without normal sensation some amputees are unable to detect changes in their body position or sense when they are at risk of losing their balance. This loss of sensation can be exacerbated when using a prosthetic limb(s) for walking which can reduce the amount of feedback received from the environment, mainly below you. One of the banes of my life is to walk on cobblestones, especially if the stones are not close together giving rise to a very uneven surface.

Many amputees experience phantom sensations whereby they feel they still have a limb where there is not one. This can be risky at night, when drowsy, as you may wake up and attempt to stand and fall, forgetting you have had an amputation. From personal experience just a few months after my amputation, when I was standing with crutches in our living room, I took a step forward without thinking. It still feels as though my leg is there both then and now, and I fell straight on the floor. Fortunately I did not hurt myself and it has never been repeated.

In addition to the loss of sensation some also experience muscle weakness, joint pain, and other physical limitations which make it more difficult to maintain balance and stability. This can be especially challenging for those who have undergone amputations of the lower limbs, as the loss of a foot or leg greatly affects the ability to walk and stand without assistance.

Your balance will be affected by the loss of a limb, whether you wear a prosthesis or not. When not wearing a prosthesis, you will obviously not be able to correct your balance by say putting your foot down. What often happens, as it did for me, was finding your ability to balance being heightened though. When wearing a prosthesis you do lose the normal sensation of your foot on the ground, therefore your balance is poor when standing or walking. The other thing adding to balance complications may be any medication needed which can also have an effect. Even having a tipple or two can have an effect.

Many amputees have diabetes which can have a huge effect on eyesight and sensation in legs. They call this lack of feeling in the legs, diabetic neuropathy, which most often damages nerves in the legs and feet. Depending on the affected nerves, diabetic neuropathy symptoms include pain and numbness in the legs, feet, and hands. It can also cause problems with the digestive system, urinary tract, blood vessels and heart. Sometimes the symptoms are mild, but it can lead to falls, as hazards may not be seen, and uneven surfaces may not be felt underfoot.

Environmental factors can also contribute to the risk of falling. Uneven surfaces obstacles like protruding drain covers, slabs slightly proud of the next are typical and other hazards can all pose a significant challenge for those with mobility issues. Even small obstacles like curbs, steps, and doorstep thresholds can be difficult to navigate and increase the risk of tripping or falling. I find the camber on some pavements difficult to walk on and these can cause me to stumble, and I must cross the road to get the reverse of the camber.

The design and layout of public spaces can also have a significant impact on the mobility of amputees in many public areas which are not designed with accessibility in mind. This makes it difficult for amputees to move around safely. For example buildings may have inaccessible entrances, restrooms, and other facilities which make it challenging to participate in public life. Living in the UK we often like to visit historic locations or buildings. Centuries ago, no thought was given to accommodate anyone with a disability. I may only see the downstairs of an historic building or castle and wait somewhere out of the way while waiting for my wife, who can access these places.

Public transportation can also be a significant challenge with many buses and trains not equipped with appropriate seating and accessibility features. I recently travelled to London by train, and on my return journey, arriving back at the station, I needed to get across a train line. Normally I would use a lift, but it had a sign stating, 'Lift Broken', and I had to use the stairs on the bridge. It was difficult for me but not insurmountable. If I had been in a wheelchair, I am unsure what would have happened. This example can be daunting to some if they are nervous about problems which they may encounter and may push them to become more insular.

There are also psychological and emotional factors that can impact the risk of falling. Fear of falling, depression, and anxiety can all contribute to a lack of confidence and an increased risk of accidents. Many amputees experience social isolation, and lack of support which can further diminish their physical and emotional well-being, all affecting confidence. There are several strategies to address the problem of falling and one of the most effective approaches is to provide education and training on safe mobility techniques and proper prosthetic use. This can help to better understand limitations and develop confidence in ability to move around safely. When first starting to use a prosthesis to walk, there is a need, and a personal requirement, to have 100% confidence in every step you take knowing it will not let you down. Having a walking aid can go a long way for this reassurance such as a frame or walking stick.

Physical therapy and exercise programmes can also be beneficial for improving strength, flexibility, and balance. These programmes can be customised to meet the needs of individuals and be tailored to address specific issues like muscle weakness, joint pain, or gait abnormalities. For me, keeping my upper body strength toned is important to supplement the loss of my leg and assist with my balance. I do a lot of things for my balance subconsciously. By just getting out of a chair or standing, I am constantly readjusting to maintain my stability.

Environmental modifications can also be helpful in reducing this risk. These may include installing handrails, ramps and other accessible features in homes and public places as well as addressing hazards like uneven flooring and tripping hazards. A must for me when I moved into a new home was to have a stair railing put in, secondly was a chair seat installed in the shower cubicle, purely to allow me to get in and out. The third thing was to have low door thresholds fitted to avoid any trip hazard this might present. Normal double glazed thresholds are not easy to step on at times, but on request, some low level ones certainly help. I always avoid rugs or slippery surfaces.

In home there are other modifications which can be made to reduce the risk of falls. This may be the installation of grab bars, handrails in bathrooms, and other areas, as well as removing trip hazards like rugs, small mats, and hanging cords. Adequate lighting should also be provided for good visibility to ensure you can see where you are going to avoid obvious or hidden obstacles. The other hidden obstacles are pets. I have two dogs who like to sleep anywhere on the floor. By that I mean they could be stretched out in front of doors. It is an obstacle course at times with them, especially if I am walking towards a door and they run in front of you because they are excited for food, walks or visitors. I would never be without them, but it does need consideration when moving around the house.

There needs to be guidance on safe mobility techniques, such as how to maintain balance on uneven surfaces and how to properly use prosthetic limbs. Even nowadays it frustrates me because there is only prosthetic training in what I call a 'clean' environment. I have said this is inadequate for the past fifty years yet still no improvement has happened. In the training centres every floor is even to walk on, unlike the big, wide world out there. There is no training given to walking on stones, cobbles, or cambers, and this can, and must be learnt after the initial training, away from the sterile environment where a physiotherapist is always close by. Having said that the physiotherapists do a first class job in building the confidence up of new amputees and provide a sterling service.

It has been suggested that in the first year after amputation over half of amputees fall. This can have devastating effects on the residual limb (stump), your mobility and confidence. To regain your new balance after amputation, and adjusting to it, takes time particularly if there are other underlying health issues. Safety is paramount because of damage which can be caused to the amputated area by a fall which can be quite a set-back in the early days. Patience is recommended, and if required the use of a wheelchair, crutches, frame, or sticks will give added confidence in mobility.

Jim - *I fell frequently, even prior to amputation. My amputation was partially the result of a fall. One day, about six years ago, I fell and landed on one of my artificial knees, (I had two at the time). Apparently, it was loosened by the fall. Later, the area developed an infection and progressed to the point of my amputation. Being diabetic did not help the situation either.*

Older people fall more frequently. Each year, millions of older people (those sixty five and older) fall. In fact, more than one out of four older people fall each year, but less than half tell their doctor. Falling once, doubles your chances of falling again.

Falls are serious and costly as can be seen below with the following USA statistical detail.

· One out of five falls causes a serious injury such as broken bones or a head injury.

· Each year, three million older people are treated in emergency departments for fall injuries.

· Over eight hundred thousand patients a year are hospitalized because of a fall injury, most often because of a head injury or hip fracture.

· Each year at least three hundred thousand older people are hospitalized for hip fractures.

· More than ninety five percent of hip fractures are caused by falling (sideways).

· In 2015, the medical costs for falls totalled more than fifty billion dollars in the United States. Medicare and Medicaid shouldered seventy five percent of these costs.

· Falls are the most common cause of traumatic brain injuries.

· Many people who fall, even if they are not injured, become afraid of falling again. This fear may cause a person to cut down on their everyday activities. When a person is less active, they become weaker, and this increases their chances of falling.

People with lower-limb loss risk accidental falls more than their non-disabled peers. A study published in 2001 found that more than fifty two percent of lower-limb amputees experience at least a fall every year, making it more than twice the rate of non-disabled elderly individuals. Researchers investigated how many individuals with limb loss have received fall training and what factors prevent its wider adoption.

The Study -

The researchers for the study developed an online questionnaire targeting people with lower-limb loss nationwide. Out of the one hundred and eighty responses, one hundred and sixty six were included in the analysis. More than two-thirds of the respondents reported not receiving fall training.

The researchers noted that considering the high incidence rate of falls among lower-limb amputees and the economic costs of falls, the numbers suggest an untapped potential in improving post-amputation care and long-term patient outcomes. The researchers also found a discrepancy in whether fall training was received and who provided it. Numerous respondents stated not receiving proper fall training but listed a provider anyway.

Among the respondents, only twenty stated they are taking tai chi or martial arts training, which have been deemed effective in helping mitigate injuries from accidental falls.

Other fall interventions -

Fall training helps individuals assess any situation and avoid falls. If falls happen, this training will provide techniques to mitigate injuries.

Fall training is comparable and compatible with other strategies, including Krav Maga, tai chi, and martial arts, to minimize the impact of falls on prosthetic users. Different methods can also help, including using the correct prosthetic components to improve balance, gait stability, and proprioception (making changes in body movement and position). In 2019, researchers found that using microprocessor knees helped increase walking speed on flat and uneven terrain, improved balance perception, and reduced accidental falls. This finding is supported by another study that found eighty two fewer falls per one hundred people with microprocessor knees.

However, the drawback of microprocessor knees is their high cost. Compared to expensive prosthetic technology, fall training costs are more reasonable. Despite the cost-effectiveness of fall training, it is still underused, wasting patients' rehabilitation potential.

Who should be responsible for fall training -

Many assume that fall training is a domain of physical therapists who provide prosthetic gait retraining and other limb-loss therapy interventions but only some prosthesis users have the means to receive physical therapy. The study highlighted that only seventy nine percent of the respondents received physical therapy. Furthermore, according to twenty seven percent of the respondents, only some physical therapy programs include proper fall training.

Although fall training does not reduce the number of accidental falls, it effectively reduces the severity of injuries from falls. In my view it is essential to bring this issue into the consciousness of a larger public, and hopefully this information will help you advocate for yourself or a loved one.

Chapter 18:

Personality Impact

The impact of amputation on someone's personality has merit in discussion because there can be both good and bad points to consider. We all have our own personality style which helps us all to be unique. Personality style in this context refers to the set of characteristics and traits which define an individual's behaviour and thoughts when a person loses a limb. It can be challenging to adjust to the physical changes associated with amputation. It is this loss which can trigger a range of emotional reactions including grief, depression, and anxiety. As a result, the individual's personality style may change in response to the loss. I do not believe mine changed but others do.

One of the most notable changes in personality style in which ageing amputees may experience is a decrease in openness. Openness is a personality trait characterised by creativity, imagination, and willingness to experience new things. In the context of amputation, a decrease in openness may be seen as a reluctance to try new activities or engage in social events as they fear judgement, or embarrassment. This shift in the personality style can lead to a reduced quality of life as the individual may feel isolated or less connected to the world around them. All of this affects the close family and circle of friends.

Another change in personality style which may be experienced is a decrease in extroversion. Extroversion is a personality trait characterised by sociability assertiveness and outgoingness. In this context a decrease may be seen as a reluctance to engage in social activities or interact with others. Almost like going into a shell. This shift in personality style can lead to reduce quality of life as the individual may feel isolated or less connected to the world around them.

It is not all negative changes in personality style which ageing amputees may experience. Many may find they become more conscientious after losing a limb. Conscientiousness is another personality trait characterised by organisational responsibility and the desire to achieve. In this context an increasing conscientiousness may be seen as a desire to adapt to their new circumstances and to engage in activities which are meaningful and fulfilling. This can lead to improved outcomes and a sense of accomplishment.

Another experience is an increase in emotional instability. This is a personality trait characterised by mood swings, anxiety, and impulsiveness. An increase in emotional instability may be seen because of the traumatic experience of losing a limb and they may experience feelings of frustration sadness, or anger, which may lead to impulsive behaviour or outbursts. This type of behaviour is very hard on the immediate family and carers.

Individuals who are narcissistically invested in their physical appearance and power, tend to react negatively to the loss of the limb. They see it as a major assault upon their dignity and self-worth. Conversely, dependent individuals may cherish the sick role and find in it a welcome relief from pressure and responsibility. It is quite amazing how each of us might, or do react to differing circumstances, and once again highlights our uniqueness as a species.

Those with a history of depression are more susceptible to a state of generalized unhappiness, restlessness, dissatisfaction, or frustration following amputation. The loss serves to crystallise notions of a basic defect, sometimes expressed in self-punishing behaviours. This is where mental health support may be required. In general, timid, and self-conscious individuals, who are excessively concerned about their social standing are more likely to suffer psychologically from limb loss than those who are self-assured individuals.

Unexpected reactions may arise from secondary gain. If disability results in improved financial or social status, psychological adjustment may be made easier, especially if those gains are not directly challenged. The first financial gain which may occur from being an amputee is employment related. Many individuals who have lost a limb may be eligible for disability benefits which can provide financial support to help cover medical expenses and lost wages. These benefits can provide financial stability for the amputee and their family during a challenging time.

Some amputees may be eligible for legal compensation if their amputation was caused by the negligence of another party. For example, if an individual last a limb due to a workplace injury or car accident they may be eligible to receive compensation for the medical expenses, lost wages, and pain and suffering. This compensation can provide significant financial support to the amputee and their family. I have met a few people like this over the years, mainly resulting from road accidents or their company's liability and it has been life changing both physically and financially. Nothing in my eyes can financially compensate for limb loss, but it can cushion the blow somewhat.

Amputation compensation claims are typically substantial, reflecting the seriousness of these types of injuries and the impact on your life. There are many companies offering to take on your case if negligence is involved because even the amputation of digits, such as a toe or fingers, can have serious consequences for the individual affected. Losing a dominant thumb, for example, is highly likely to make using that hand much more difficult, and you may have to learn to write again.

When looking at the compensation payments there are many aspects to consider. These include: -

- **Medical Expenses** - An amputation can require considerable medical care, including surgeries, hospital stays, rehabilitation, and assistive devices. Compensation for medical expenses can cover these costs, including future medical expenses related to the amputation. Although in the UK much of this is covered by the National Health Service there are still private companies offering more individual help, at a cost.

- **Lost Wages** - An amputee may not be able to work in their previous occupation, resulting in a loss of income. Compensation for lost wages can include past and future lost wages, as well as a loss of earning capacity.

- **Property Damage** - If the amputation was the result of an accident, the victim may have suffered property damage, such as a motorbike or car. Compensation for property damage can cover the cost of repairing or replacing any damaged property.

- **Pain and Suffering** - Amputation can cause immense physical pain and emotional distress. Compensation for this pain and suffering can also be sought.

- **Loss of Enjoyment of Life** - An amputation can limit a person's ability to engage in activities they previously enjoyed. Compensation for loss of enjoyment of life can cover the inability to participate in activities and hobbies due to the amputation.

- **Punitive Damages** - Punitive damages refer to compensation awarded to punish the person or entity responsible for the amputation. These damages are typically only awarded in cases of intentional harm or extreme negligence.

Not every amputation is the result of negligence, it may just be the luck of the draw which nature dealt you. I have often thought about my own personal circumstances with the consultant telling me it was psychological, and I was trying to get off school. Was this negligent on his part or was it just a fundamental lack of knowledge about my type of rare cancer at the time? Many years ago there were not the specialised law firms dealing with negligence, and besides which I had a poor background where any litigation approach was financially prohibitive. The 'No Win, No Fee' basis was not even thought of then!

Some people may be eligible for specialised employment programmes which cater for individuals with disabilities, such as vocational rehabilitation. These programmes help with job training, education, and job placement. This could enable finding work, which is well suited to the individual's abilities, and ensure financial stability in the long term. Another financial gain that may occur from being an amputee is access to financial assistance programmes and resources. Many organisations and foundations offer financial assistance programmes to individuals with disabilities. These programmes may provide financial assistance with medical expenses, adaptive equipment, and transportation.

Jim - *Psychologists define personality as a person's distinctive patterns of thinking, feeling, and behaving. Personality is a mix of innate dispositions and inclinations along with environmental factors and experiences. It encompasses all the thoughts, behaviour patterns, and social attitudes which impact how we view ourselves and what we believe about others and the world around us. Personality is relatively stable over long time periods, but it changes over the entire lifetime, especially as we get older.*

I have heard many people say that an amputation changes your personality. As a result of my interaction with many other amputees, I have concluded the range of amputee personality types is not any different than the general population. However, since I did not know these amputees prior to their amputations, I cannot confirm if their personalities changed or not. They may have changed from a positive personality to the negative group, but so do people who are not amputees. Life has a way of changing all of us. The important thing is how we deal with it.

Personally, I do not think my personality has changed much since my amputation. I have conscientiously worked very hard at trying not to let outside factors and influences change my personality, attitudes, behaviours toward others, sense of humour, or my, 'Just deal with it' attitude. I believe we have two personalities: our inner, private personality and our public personality. How many times have you heard someone say, 'He or she has a (insert adjective here) personality.' You determine how others perceive your personality but the one that really counts is your inner, private one and is the one you can control.

In my opinion, the two major factors which can affect your attitude and reflect in your personality are pain and mobility. I am very, very lucky when it comes to pain. I do not have any phantom pain. If I did, most of my comments would be entirely different. The pains I experience are what can be expected when you are in your eighties. Based on comments I see on social media; I can see how frequent pain will cause personality changes in people which includes amputees and non-amputees.

Mobility is another story. Early on after amputation, my goal was to regain mobility. After fighting with poor fitting sockets for more than five years, and declining mobility, I have decided to adapt and stop sticking a sharp stick in my eye. My remaining years will be free of the frustration of physically fighting sockets and walkers. I am still able to navigate, drive a car, and get from point A to B with reasonable effort using a wheelchair. If I was thirty-five, I would still be fighting.

Chapter 19:

Declining Mobility

How foolish many of us are when we are young and feel invincible. Even as a teenage amputee it was a reality check having cancer so young for me. My so-called invincibility was shattered into a thousand pieces when I was told I needed to have my whole right leg amputated. I have therefore, all my life appreciated how fortunate I have been with good health. It is only now in the autumn years of my life you feel the ravages of time a little more. The aches and pains from too much exercising or physical activity instead of disappearing a few hours or days later just linger a little longer. Then those aches and pains end up staying as the years' role by, such is life.

I think as we age externally and all of us slow down our internal age clock with such wonderful imagination. This makes us think as if we are still in the prime of our lives at twenty or thirty odd years of age. Maybe it is a coping mechanism, but the mirror is a reality check.

I have always looked at life as being a gift, which contrasts with those who negatively think life is a burden. Although I understand the extremes some face and believe myself to be fortunate in comparison to some poor souls. Whilst recently watching a programme on the pop singer Roy Orbison I thought about the life he had. It was one of initial struggle, from a poor upbringing to try and establish himself as a singer and composer. His wife died in his arms after a motorbike accident, she was only twenty seven years old. Just eighteen months later he lost two of his children in a house fire while he was on tour. Many lows and highs in a life well lived with some tremendous songs as his legacy. In the programme he demonstrated his wisdom to me by saying, "My voice is a gift, my talent is a gift, the life process is a gift, the opportunity for the journey is a gift". What a journey he had.

If you are a single leg amputee there is quite a strain on your existing knee and hip. I never thought too much in my 'invincible' years until a few strange aches, twinges and pain started in my mid-forties. The slight dull ached experienced in my 'good', left hip, remembering part of my right pelvis was removed during my amputation, first appeared. It was nothing too much but has very slowly returned every few months over many years with a gradual pain increase. It does not stay too long, so it is currently manageable. Other things hurt much more! The bigger problem was my 'good' knee. It started with a dull ache but seemed most acute when using the stairs. I go up or down two steps at a time, but it was coming down where the pain was progressively getting worse.

One of my previous jobs was working on huge £900M railway project for Westinghouse in Chippenham. The offices were in several huge two story buildings alongside a large car park. The stairs to the top where I worked were longer than the normal ones. The only lift was an external industrial lift not one you could easily use, as it needed someone to work it. One day as I was walking down the steps one evening to get to my car in the car park, I got to within four or five steps from the bottom to the exit door when the pain was so extreme, I could go no further. I was sweating with the pain and waited nearly ten minutes for it to subside before attempting the few steps left. It was a wakeup call to better manage my body.

I moved to another role at British Energy in Cheltenham where they had several lifts. I always used these lifts rather than stairs and I had no repeat of the previous knee problem. I have done this ever since and use stairs or escalators whenever or wherever I can. The knee problem I experienced culminated in a knee arthroscopy and then smoothing back the worn lining of the cartilage. It worked and because of this keyhole surgery I was able to be back walking in a few days.

There is tremendous pressure on your knees when descending stairs so it is important to manage as best you can your own weight. Think of your knee as a fulcrum and at one point all your weight is on that pivot point. Tremendous forces are at play, so fitness is a key factor to ensure a longer, mobile life.

Since I have retired my mobility has decreased. There is a two-fold reason for this. Firstly at work there is more walking every day than just being at home, and I now do not need to force myself to walk anywhere unnecessary, remembering for me, every step is painful. Secondly there have been issues with my prosthesis, which to a degree has limited how much walking I can do. It has been several years since I have had a 'spare' leg, should I need it. Couple this with the general ageing process and thinning of the skin, which has increased the phantom pains, and it helps explain some of my limited mobility.

For some, declining mobility can be linked to a poorer quality of life. There can be an impact on employment and personal relationships, but this is the negative aspect of amputation and there is another more positive side to see. Many have a loving relationship where life transitioning has been needed and supported by partners and close family. This decline can also be associated with the physical ailments brought on by ageing, pain, and even mental health problems.

Unless congenital, the loss of a limb is progressive and degenerative. With this comes the effect of comorbidities, often in older age, which to the layman means the simultaneous presence of two or more diseases or medical conditions. It is difficult enough managing on a day-to-day basis being an amputee let alone numerous other debilitating health issues. If you consider this further, whether ex-services or not, there is a substantial cost and financial commitment required in caring for amputees throughout their lifetime to safeguard their long-term health and care needs.

I was recently asked what my thoughts were on losing may leg at sixteen or later in life, say in your sixties. There are several aspects to it, but I do believe for me it was best to lose my leg at a young age as I was still growing and maturing so transitioning was easier had I been in my sixties. The other aspect is often there are several other medical issues being faced as you get older, and the impact of amputation is compounded by these.

In ageing, some of the more usual health problems result from a history of heart and stroke problems. Common health conditions such as arthritis and diabetes do not always mean decreased mobility. I have seen first-hand where the patient is just not suitable for a prosthesis and will never use it.

Some arrive in a wheelchair and when fitted with a prosthesis struggle to stand upright while wearing it and taking one or two steps requires a huge amount of effort on their part. Given one of the tools to successful use of a prosthesis is confidence, if you can only walk one or two steps then confidence can take a long time to pin down. With every step taken you do need 100% confidence the prosthesis will not let you down.

Some older amputees like to use a four wheel stroller, or three wheel rollator when starting to walk. A 'Zimmer frame' is another alternative. From my own perspective when I see them walking, they mostly seem to lean forward in them to grip the handles. This somewhat stooped posture is not good when learning to walk. Although I can understand the need for confidence in not falling over when taking a few steps, it does not allow the correct walking motion one should adopt for improved mobility. This of course must be measured with what can best be achieved in the short-term and the use of an aid, after consideration may always be necessary.

The anxiety and panic experienced by some older people is often taken into consideration when assessing suitability for using a lower limb prosthesis. Often it can be too daunting a challenge both mentally and physically. It is just a case by case review and ongoing assessment.

The simple fact is you cannot stop the ageing process. As much as we do not like it, the inevitable will happen. We can slow it down by keeping fit and on the move as much as we are able to as this will always help. Not too many lazy people live a long life!

Genes will always play a part in longevity, but this is always balanced with the lifestyle lived. From being young and fearless, to the more mature and pragmatic, is one of life's strange enigmas with the saying, 'You cannot put an old head on young shoulders', which is so true.

From a personal perspective I retired at sixty five. Bren and I had many holidays both abroad and, in the UK, especially using the newly acquired motorhome. It was not only the motorhome, but two dogs as well which have brought so much fun into our lives. I was not as active as I used to be at work because meetings, deadlines to make, and staff issues were now a thing of the past. It was the joy of retirement where I could or could not do things. There were choices. Then Covid hit us all, and lockdowns were enforced. All these things impacted me, and I knew my mobility had decreased. The one other aspect affecting me significantly was my prosthesis, it was not as easy to walk with as I had found in the past. As all amputees know, no two legs are made the same. For several years I have had only one artificial leg which I wear day in, day out.

My spare leg has just been completed but I am told the style I use is now redundant and no spare parts are available. Fortunately I found an old hip locking mechanism given to me a few years ago which they salvaged to complete the leg. This is disastrous for me personally as I do not want to start learning to walk on a completely new style of leg after using the same type for many, many years. Some simple forward planning on this and procurement of spare parts would not have cost too much and mean so much for the patient. Unfortunately the world is run by accountants and decisions made are black and white with nothing in between. I have always said common sense is uncommon.

One other thing I did was to buy a couple of mobility scooters. It was a big decision for me personally because of my own 'hang-ups' about hiding my disability as much as I can. Having a mobility scooter gives a label of disability, hence my problem. I had one for general use and the other for putting in the car or motorhome. The latter breaks down into five pieces and can be put into the boot of the car and transported. By swallowing my own issues and listening to Bren about this I was able to go out with her when she walked the dogs. I do try not to be lazy, but it can make you that way inclined when it is so easy to get on a scooter. The balance for me is scooter equals mobility with no pain, whereas walking, to be mobile, equals pain. I was now also able to be with Bren and share so many happy, memorable moments, which I hope to continue.

I remember how I felt making this decision and had read, 'As long as you know who you are and what makes you happy, it does not matter how others see you.'. It was a thought provoking statement I never forgot.

With declining mobility, isolation is also a factor to consider. If you are fortunate to have a strong family unit and they are close by to support you, it can help enormously. This applies to all able and disabled people as the ageing process advances. Whether the isolation is a result of a reluctance to wear a prosthesis or even not having a carer/family member to take you outside the home in a wheelchair which can also be an issue.

Mobility is the key to independence and with ageing, other illnesses can complicate this, making it challenging. It has been suggested that elderly amputees are at greater risk of psychiatric disturbances like depression moreso than others. If their interpersonal relationships are difficult or in some cases non-existent this can also be exacerbated by any functional capacity which they might have.

I can understand taking the easy road and not do anything or go out anywhere, but it is a bad habit to start. Those who experienced the Covid shutdowns, once the novelty of this wore thin, realised that humans like and need to interact. Even being outside stimulates our sensory needs and helps towards a feeling of well-being. I know I missed going out and understood 'cabin fever' a little more, which in turn has given an appreciation of 'mindfulness' too. Sometimes the simple things can be the most stimulating, like looking very closely at a flower or just closing your eyes in a forest to hear the birds or wind blowing through the leaves.

As we age, our declining mobility may be due to natural wear and tear. In my case I have arthritis in my good knee and hip. I can manage it when it flares up with medication, but it is progressively getting worse. Many amputees as they age have concerns about hip and knee replacements and if it did happen, what is the recovery time for getting back to a weight bearing norm. For myself if a hip replacement was necessary, I would be unable to wear my prosthesis for some time especially as the belt around my good hip is weight bearing when I walk. A possibility I shudder at!

There are many considerations, but we should not forget those less fortunate than ourselves not living in the UK, who do not have the luxury of the National Health or some form of health insurance. For them any major surgery is far more drastic and life changing. We should count our blessings.

An example mentioned to me was in Tasmania where an amputee lady in her seventies became wheelchair bound and no accessible accommodation could be found for her. The only accessible accommodation she could find was 250km away and was for university students. At this ripe old age she has started an undergraduate degree, whereby the university supply wheelchair accessible housing. I would say desperate times equals desperate measures.

Closer to home and something we all do is occasionally use the bathroom during the night. For me I just get out of bed and hop to the bathroom, but others cannot do this and worry for the future and what it holds. Some use a walker or Zimmer frame, whereas others use a wheelchair or a commode. The worse part for all of us is losing your independence and the reliance on family or helpers. No-one wants to be a burden to others, but at times we all need a little help. If you are isolated without any support, it can be a desolate, concerning time.

People facing amputation in later life are naturally focussed on the operation itself and the trauma around it. What little consideration is given to the longer term impact is something put to the back of the mind and not thought about until the current events are long past. It is for this reason, 'Support Groups' are important to get feedback from the 'horse's mouth' rather than able bodied 'expert' theoretical advice.

I think the timeframe of amputation is important in consideration of your declining mobility. If you were born without a limb(s) then it has just been the norm all your life. If it happens in the early part of your life, like me, then I feel happy to have at least experienced being fully able bodied and able to enjoy everything it brings. You are young enough to adapt to a new way of living. Having a prosthesis at an early age must have some ageing health issues in which the confines and unnatural walking the body must adopt causes varying degrees of scoliosis or other wear issues as the years progress.

One other consideration is the weight of the prosthesis. A below knee one weighs three or four pounds (2kg) or like mine weighs fourteen pound (6.5kg). This weight detrimentally compounds the effect on the body over time.

Mid-life amputees face other adjustments especially within the family circle and this can test fragile relationships. Again the long term ageing process is not an instant issue because of the immediate adjustment in life to being an amputee. Mobility reduction is of course dependent upon the nature of the amputation, the height of the amputation and the number of limbs.

Later-life amputees are faced with not only the major trauma of limb amputation but often the cause or causes can be a serious health consideration too compounding the circumstances of surgery. This of course can greatly impact the road to recovery and their ability to use a prosthesis. For doctors and health support workers it is a serious consideration for what is best for the patient.

Jim - *My comments are directed more to U. S. amputees but hopefully will be enlightening to those who live in other countries.*

For amputees in the USA there are two distinct roles mobility takes on. There is the physical and emotional side of mobility but also a political and financial one too.
This is the side where they use your degree of mobility to determine the amount of financial assistance you will be receiving from Medicare, and private insurance companies who follow the requirements of Medicare to determine their contribution toward your prosthetic equipment. It all depends upon your ability to ambulate at various levels. From being unable to walk, to being a Paralympian.

The process of moving through the progressions from amputation, healing, then rehabilitation, physical and occupational therapy and on to decisions regarding what type of prosthetics best meet our needs is a long, physically, and mentally laborious one. What people like me did not realize is at the end of that trail awaits the challenge of dealing with Medicare or the insurance companies who are going to require you to demonstrate to their satisfaction you need all that expensive durable medical equipment (DME) to function.

For an exceedingly long time, amputee advocates, like the prosthetic manufacturers, orthopedic surgeons, certified prosthetists, therapists and groups like the Amputee Coalition and others have argued prosthetic equipment should not be in the same general DME categories such as wheelchairs, crutches, hospital beds, for reimbursement. The view is their classification is the same as other replacement devices attached to the body like artificial knees, hips, shoulders, pacemakers, stents, and hearts. Need a new hip? No problem if your doctor says so. Want a microprocessor knee? Better be able to physically demonstrate it by taking one or more standardized tests to prove you qualify and need it.

No one told me about this next statement or how I needed to demonstrate my mobility to get what equipment I needed to function at an acceptable level. I thought it would be like just going to a store and picking out what I thought I needed. This was the biggest mistake of my whole amputation experience.

The bottom line is you need to do everything you can, both pre and post amputation, to get yourself in the best physical shape you can so you have the mobility, strength, and stamina to perform at your ability level to maximize the chances of getting the level of equipment you need to live the way you want to live. As ageing seniors, this is much more difficult than if you were thirty years old. In my view, you need to decide the price you are willing to pay based on your physical condition and mobility goals.

When my amputation occurred at age seventy-eight, I was determined to leap tall buildings. I was able to get qualified at the K-3 Level helped by creative documentation by my doctor and certified prosthetist. Now, I am in my eighties and after more than five years of setbacks and poor mobility, I am willing to use my wheelchair and take the elevator to the top floor and just admire the scenery!

K-levels are a rating system used by Medicare and insurance companies to indicate an amputee's rehabilitation potential. The system is a rating from zero through to four, and it indicates a person's potential to use a prosthetic device. K-level designation is important because it is one of the determining factors in the decision of componentry which may be a decision made by the prosthetist for the prosthetic device and paid for by Medicare and other insurance companies.

There are a total of five levels (K-levels = 0 to 4), and Medicare defines them as follows:

- K-0 The patient does not have the ability or potential to ambulate or transfer safely with or without assistance and a prosthesis does not enhance their quality of life or mobility.
- K-1 The patient has the ability or potential to use a prosthesis for transfers or ambulation on level surfaces at fixed cadence or speed. This is typical of a household ambulator or a person who only walks in their own home.
- K-2 The patient has the ability or potential for ambulation with the ability to traverse low-level environmental barriers such as curbs, stairs, or uneven surfaces. This is typical of the limited community ambulator.
- K-3 The patient has the ability or potential for ambulation with variable cadence or multiple speeds. A person at level 3 is typically a community ambulator who can traverse most environmental barriers and may have vocational, therapeutic or exercise activity that demands prosthetic use beyond simple locomotion.
- K-4 The patient has the ability or potential for prosthetic ambulation that exceeds basic ambulation skills, exhibiting high impact, stress, or energy levels. This is typical of the prosthetic demands of the child, active adult, or athlete.
- How are K-levels determined? K-levels are determined by the clinician (prosthetist, therapist, or physician), using one of the following commonly used outcome measures. Amputee Mobility Predictor (AMP) Patient Assessment Validation Evaluation Test (PAVET) Prosthesis Evaluation Questionnaire (PEQ) Timed Up and Go (TUG) Timed Walk Tests Distance Walk.

Typically, it takes months of back-and-forth negotiation between your team and the company before an agreement on what they will pay.

The other elephant in the room is the Federal Drug Administration (FDA). It can take years before approving innovative technology to help us. For instance, osseointegration surgery in which the USA is ten years behind certain European countries in getting it available. For years, people went to Europe or Australia to have the procedure done!

Chapter 20:

Amputation Ghosting

Whilst on a social media website recently, which was associated with those suffering or who have suffered from cancer, someone used the word 'cancer ghosting', and I thought after reading this the same scenario applied to amputation. When people are interacting with someone who has been diagnosed with cancer, many often find themselves at a loss for words, and contact unexpectedly ceases. I found this happened years ago when one girlfriend came to see me, but never came back again. It was such a surreal situation and one she, or even I no doubt, had ever thought would experience, and we were totally unprepared for it.

There are analogies which spring to mind when discussing amputation, like cancer, or even death, which is why some people suffer the grieving process after losing a limb. In my day there was little or no preparation for amputation or even post-amputation, you just got on with it. Thanks goodness times have changed, and we have moved forward.

In putting more meat on the words 'Amputation Ghosting', it is where people just do not know what you need or even what they should say. They are willing to help but feel uncomfortable. Often if someone is speaking openly about their forthcoming amputation or prosthetic then they are probably open to questions and a discussion. If they are not, then the response or reaction might be difficult hence the awkwardness of the situation.

Amputation is a complex and highly personal issue which affects many millions of people around the world. However when it comes to interacting with someone who is facing this, many people often find themselves at a loss for words. There are several reasons why people do not know what to say to someone facing this, including the fear of saying the wrong thing. Also discomfort with discussing medical issues, and a lack of understanding, or even no experience of the implication of amputation can be quite difficult.

One common reason why people struggle to know what to say to someone facing this is akin to walking on eggshells. Amputation is often associated with negative emotions such as loss and grief, and they may be afraid of saying something insensitive or hurtful. They may also feel pressure to say exactly the right thing to provide comfort and support to the person, which can be a daunting task especially if the person they are talking to is highly sensitive or emotional about the matter. Sometimes people avoid meeting at all, such is their dilemma.

People may not know what to say because they feel uncomfortable discussing medical issues. After all amputations are a medical procedure which involves the removal of a part or whole of the limb which many people may not be familiar with by way of terminology and the procedures involved. This discomfort can make it difficult to engage in meaningful conversation and provide empathetic support to someone facing this.

Amputation affects each person in a unique way. People who have not experienced this themselves or had a close friend or family member face amputation may not have a frame of reference for understanding the emotions and challenges that come with it. It can be challenging to know what to say to someone facing this procedure, but it is still possible to provide meaningful support and compassion. One of the best approaches is to simply listen and offer empathy, letting the person know you are there to support them, and you understand it is a challenging time. By offering practical assistance, such as helping with household tasks, or transportation to medical appointments, may be a start to the help and supportive process.

It is also important to educate yourself about amputation, and the experiences of those who have faced it before. This can help you better understand the challenges and emotions which come with this which enables you to provide better support to someone facing this issue.

This hits at the very heart of disability awareness and the huge learning curve we all need to be on. A great way to teach children about disabilities is by talking about the daily impact it can have on people's lives. For example, I would be quite happy to talk about my disability and the impact of amputation and its effect on my life. Disability awareness is an important part of establishing inclusion for people with disability. Often our fears and discomfort about interacting with people with disability is based on lack of knowledge, uncertainties, and stereotypes that can influence attitudes.

It is not just children who need educating but some adults too. Even in the modern world we live in where information is just at the tip of your fingertips, it is still unfortunately necessary to re-educate some. As children we were instilled with common manners, decency and an appreciation of someone else's privacy and space, which seems to be sorely lacking in society today. This is why education is so important. This training helps to educate around core aspects of disability and disability related issues, giving people greater confidence when engaging with friends, family, and work colleagues. Recognising and respecting differences in others and treating everyone like you want them to treat you, will help make our world a better place for everyone to enjoy and evolve as a caring society.

Jim - *"Ghosting" is a new term often used by social media users. Its use was to describe the practice of ending a personal relationship with someone by suddenly and without explanation withdrawing from all communication. This has now spread to describe other situations where people tend to disconnect with each other about things which are uncomfortable or hard to deal with. People tend to shy away from those things which they do not understand and consequently do not know how to manage. They then try to distance themselves from the uncomfortable situation as much as possible.*

Most people have had a good friend or a best mate, before our amputation. After amputation, we saw less and less of them and finally, they fell off the face of the earth, never seen again. Whose fault is that? My belief is it is our fault! Not because we had an amputation, but because we did not take the initiative and reach out and communicate with our best friend, both pre and post-amputation. We could help them understand what we are dealing with and how they can help us continue to live our lives in the best, modified way. Let them know it is acceptable to joke about it, or not. Make them feel comfortable with you again. I have found if you make people feel comfortable with you, they will bend over backwards to help you. In my view our job is to create an environment where people understand us, and you will be amazed by the results. They expect you to be down in the dumps, and if you are, 'Fake It Till You Make It!' Granted, for months after surgery you are not in the mood to speak much to most people, but you do need to communicate with people, especially your family.

I have found attitudes are rapidly changing in a positive direction, not only toward amputees but also toward people with all kinds of other disabilities. This change, fuelled by increased awareness and communication in advertising as well as social media and various special interest groups and organizations. People have found that it is OK to talk about what were previously uncomfortable topics. I remember as a young child my maternal relatives would never say the word, 'Cancer.' In hushed tones, they referred to it as 'C.' They would say something like, "It is so sad. He has 'C.'

Today, there are very few taboos related to previously uncomfortable subjects. We have TV ads on every medical condition under the sun, which in the past would not have happened. There are more intentional highlighting of issues dealing with disabilities than ever before and that has opened the channels of communication. Education and factual knowledge shine a light on a previously dark place. The more a person knows about the various facets of amputation life, the more likely they will be willing to discuss what they previously felt uncomfortable discussing.

I do not have a problem with 'Ghosting,' because I cannot think of anyone who has 'Ghosted' me. I have broadened my circle of friends and contacts by connecting with other amputees through amputee social media groups and other support groups which are available on amputee organizations web sites. Here again, the point is you need to take the initiative! Reach out and touch someone which is how I wound up writing comments for John's book. We connected through a mutual social media friend, and John was looking for people to add comments of personal experience to his book and I responded. Again, I repeat you need to take the initiative!

Chapter 21:

Choices

Life is about choices. The choices we make have an impact on our future and the way we choose to live our lives. These choices can be as small as deciding what to eat for breakfast, or as significant as choosing a career path and life partner. Even the decision to have an amputation may arise, like myself at sixteen. My choice being to have an amputation or die!

Mobility choices play a significant role in the life of an amputee. They can choose to use a wheelchair, crutches, or other mobility aids, or they may choose to use a prosthetic limb. The decision depends on the level of amputation, physical health, mental health, and lifestyle. Wheelchairs may be the most practical option for some, while others may prefer the independence and mobility provided by prosthetics. It is choices again!

Rehabilitation choices are also very important, which include choices to undergo physical therapy, occupational therapy, or both. Physical therapy is crucial for rebuilding strength, flexibility, and mobility. Occupational therapy focuses on improving daily living skills, such as dressing, cooking, and personal care. The choice of rehabilitation depends on the level of amputation, overall health, and personal goals.

In addition to physical choices, self-perception and mental health are also a critical aspect of life. Amputees may have to choose to accept their new body image, seek counselling or support groups, or undergo cosmetic surgery. These choices can have a significant impact on the mental health, self-esteem, and overall quality of life.

One of the most important choices we make in life is the decision that shapes our future. These choices can be career choices, which determine our occupation, income, and financial stability. They can also be personal choices, which affect our relationships, family, and social life.

Furthermore, they can be choices about health, which determine lifestyle, habits, and overall well-being.

An amputee must make several health choices to maintain their physical and mental well-being. These choices have a significant impact on daily life, rehabilitation, general living, and long term health.

A balanced diet is essential for maintaining a healthy weight and overall fitness. Foods chosen should be high in nutrients, vitamins and minerals which support recovery and prevent any nutritional deficiencies. Adjustment to diet may be required to accommodate any physical limitations such as changes in appetite. food preparation, or ability to cook.

Exercise and physical activity are also crucial for maintaining physical health. Regular exercise can help build muscle strength, maintain flexibility, and reduce the risk of cardiovascular diseases. The type and intensity of exercise or physical activity depend on the level of amputation and overall health. Low impact activities like swimming, cycling, and walking are often recommended, which is of course dependent on the severity of amputation.

Amputees may need to adapt their lifestyle to accommodate their physical limitations. This may include modifications to their living environment, work environment, and leisure activities. Modifications such as handrails, ramps, and wheelchair friendly access can improve accessibility and safety. There is no benefit in being stubborn about not having these modifications if they make for a more comfortable, safer environment and help avoid potential downstream complications through injury.

Proper wound and skin care are critical for preventing infections and other medical complications. It is important to both clean and inspect the stump and report any signs of inflammation or infection to their doctor. Adequate stump care can prevent skin breakdown and reduce the risk of phantom limb pain.

Amputees should be mindful of their mental health, adjusting to a new body image and lifestyle can be challenging and result in depression, anxiety, or other mental health issues. Amputees should also address any mental health concerns with their doctor and seek help from family, friends, or support groups.

It is important to stay up to date with medical appointments, including regular checkouts, physical therapy, and follow up appointments with their prosthetist. Regular monitoring can help identify any medical issues early on and prevent complications. All these are choices along life's way and making wrong choices will lead to consequences. My motto is to never have to say, 'If only'. You need to work hard at making the right choices.

It is therefore essential to make well informed choices, considering the pros and cons, and the potential outcome of our choices. We must be aware of the consequences of each decision, and we should think carefully about the long term effects. Sometimes it can be easy to make choices based on our immediate desires, but we must think about the bigger picture and what we want for our future.

Life choices can also be influenced by the people around us. Family, friends, and society can shape decisions and affect our future. This is because amputees often require a strong support system to help them cope with the changes in their lives, after all amputation is a traumatic experience. It is essential to be aware of the influence of others and to take responsibility for the choices made. We must be aware of our own values and beliefs to make the best decisions for ourselves.

One way in which people can influence life choices is through their attitudes towards disability. If the people around have a negative attitude towards disabilities, then they might feel ashamed and embarrassed about their amputation. They might choose to hide their prosthetic limb or avoid situations where their amputation might be visible. On the other hand, if people around have a positive attitude towards disabilities, the amputee might feel empowered and confident. They might choose to embrace their prosthetic limb and actively seek out opportunities to show it off.

Another way in which people can influence life choices is through their expectations. If the people around have low expectations of what they can achieve, they might feel discouraged and unmotivated. They might choose to limit their goals and aspirations and settle for a less fulfilling life.

Conversely if people around have high expectations, they might feel motivated and determined to succeed. They might choose to set ambitious goals and work hard to achieve them.

Family members can also play a significant role in shaping life choices. If they are supportive and encouraging, the amputee is more likely to thrive. They may choose to pursue education, or career goals which might not have otherwise been considered. My father always wanted me to have an apprenticeship, which I assume was a form of security because he came through the 'Great Depression' in the 1930's, leaving an indelible mark on his concerns. After my amputation I changed my job three times until I settled down with my fourth job for twenty seven years. My father was always supportive of my decisions, but I know he always worried about me having a secure job, although recognising he was born into a different, changing time than me. He was always trying to be helpful and supportive.

Well supported amputees might also feel more confident about forming relationships and starting a family of their own. However if their family members are unsupportive, or dismissive of their amputation, they might feel isolated and alone. They might even struggle to form meaningful connections with others and might not be able to make the most of their potential. In some cases in some cultures there can be stigma to someone having an amputation resulting in them being ostracized. The family must be crucial in these instances.

Healthcare professionals can also influence amputee life choices. If they treat them with respect and empathy, they are more likely to feel confident and optimistic about their future. They might choose to follow their advice and take an active role in their rehabilitation. However if they are dismissive or uninterested in their needs, they might feel like their challenges are being overlooked. They might also be less likely to engage in their rehabilitation and may not make the progress they need to live a fulfilling life. My mind goes back to my school days and the subjects I liked and disliked, which as times were influenced by the teacher for the subjects being taught. We can be knowingly or unknowingly be influenced positively or negatively.

Life is a journey, and we can always make changes and decisions along the way. I call them crossroads along the road we travel, and the choice we make for the route we take. It is not a problem to make mistakes and learn from them, and it is acceptable to change our minds and make different choices. We should not be afraid to take risks and pursue our dreams, even if it may mean making difficult choices.

When something bad happens, like an amputation, you have three choices. You can either let it define you, let it destroy you, or let it strengthen you. The choice is yours!.

Jim - My comments will pertain to one aspect of making choices. I have only been an amputee for seven percent of my time on the planet! The other ninety-three percent I spent living a lifestyle that contributed to me becoming an amputee! Eat, drink and be merry for tomorrow you will be overweight, develop diabetes, and vascular problems, eventually end up with the loss of your right leg above the knee and potentially part of the left one too! This is what happened to me. Numerous famous people, including Mickey Mantle and Mae West have claimed to have originated the quote, 'If I had known I would have lived this long, I would have taken better care of myself.' This is fitting for me!

Lower-limb amputations (LLA), which is surgery to remove a toe, foot, or leg, are increasing in the US. Currently, about 200,000 people in the United States have amputations each year, and about 160,000 of those amputations are a result of complications from diabetes. From 2009 to 2019, the number of diabetes-related hospitalisations due to amputation doubled, but the good news is most diabetes-related amputations may not have happened with lifestyle changes, blood sugar management, regular foot checks, and prompt wound care when needed. The message of this story is if you are diabetic or pre-diabetic, it needs to be under control!

Unfortunately, many of us reading this are already diabetic so our mission is to spread the message of how serious diabetes can be. Educate your family and friends about this killer. The situation in the UK is similar and while the numbers are not as large, the number of major lower limb amputations in diabetes continues to rise with seven thousand nine hundred and fifty seven major diabetic lower limb amputations in England reported between 2017 to 2020.

Chapter 22:

Cosmetic Appearance for Amputees

There will be many views on this subject because we are all individuals with our own views on how we feel being an amputee, and disabled. Even the word 'disabled' is emotive and perhaps the word should be 'enabled'. Cosmetic appearance is an important aspect for many individuals including those who have undergone amputation. Losing a limb can be a traumatic experience and the cosmetic appearance of a prosthetic limb can often play a crucial role in the overall acceptance of the new physical state. What most amputees want is to have the most realistic and aesthetically pleasing prosthetic limb, whilst others want to make a statement.

As amputees know, the loss of a limb can be a challenging and life altering experience for anyone. It can affect an individual's self-esteem, confidence, and overall quality of life. While prosthetic technology has come a long way in recent years, aesthetic considerations are often just as important as functional ones. A prosthetic limb which looks realistic and aesthetically pleasing can help some feel more comfortable and confident in their new bodies. The new limb over time does become an integral part of you. I would however add, one of life's pleasures for me, is at the end of a hard day, to remove my prosthesis and feel free of it.

One of the first considerations when it comes to the cosmetic appearance of prosthetics is to colour match. Typically prosthetic limbs come in a range of skin tone colours to match the individuals remaining limb. This is an essential aspect, as it can significantly affect the overall appearance of the prosthetic limb. A mismatched colour can be a constant reminder of the amputation and it can make individuals feel self-conscious about their appearance. When I first had my prosthesis there was only one colour, and that was a dark pink! It felt like Henry Ford, who said when he started producing model T cars, 'A customer can have a car painted any colour he wants, as long as it's black.'

Another area of importance when it comes to cosmetic appearance is the shape and size of the prosthetic limb. It is crucial the prosthetic limb is proportionate to the individuals remaining limb. An oversized or undersized prosthetic can lead to an unnatural appearance which can make individuals feel uncomfortable and self-conscious. Therefore proper measurements and fitting of the prosthetic limb are essential to ensure the best possible fit and appearance. I can relate to this because recently the fairing on my prosthesis must have been replaced with a much slimmer one, when compared to my actual leg. I am unsure how or even why this happened, and I did not notice it until I arrived home. I had to wait several months to get it replaced and during this time was acutely aware how different it looked when I was sat down.

The materials used in the prosthetic limb can also play a crucial role in its aesthetics. I remember how pleased I was to have a sponge fairing, which felt more like a real leg than the one I had for years made from aluminium. Many prosthetics nowadays are made of silicone or other material that mimic the look and feel of skin, this can provide a more realistic appearance, which can help increase the confidence and acceptance of the missing limb. In addition to being comfortable to wear, prosthetic limbs made of these materials can also be custom made to match the individuals skin tone.

Cosmetic considerations are not limited to the prosthetic limb itself but also extend to the prosthetic socket. The socket is the part of the prosthetic limb that attaches to the individual's residual limb. It is essential that the socket is fitted correctly and is comfortable to wear as it is the foundation of the prosthetic limb. A well fitted socket can also contribute to the overall appearance of the prosthetic limb by creating a seamless transition between the prosthetic and the individuals remaining limb.

Cosmetic tattoos for amputees have gained popularity in recent times, partly due to advances in technology and growing awareness about them. These tattoos are designed to enhance the appearance of amputated limbs in providing a sense of completeness and wholeness to the individuals who have undergone amputation. The tattoos can also help to conceal scars and other skin blemishes thus improving the overall appearance of the affected area.

One of the key benefits of cosmetic tattoos for amputees is that they can help to restore a sense of balance and symmetry to the body. Amputations can cause significant changes to the body's appearance leading to feelings of self-consciousness and even shame. By adding tattoos to the affected area, individuals can visually complete the limb and reduce the appearance of amputation. This can be particularly beneficial in cases where the amputation was sudden or traumatic as it can help to promote a sense of acceptance and healing.

Another way cosmetic tattoos can enhance the appearance of amputees is by helping to conceal scars or other skin blemishes. Amputation surgery can leave behind significant scarring which can be both unsightly and emotionally distressing for the individual. By adding tattoos to the area, the scars can be camouflaged, making them less visible and less likely to draw attention. This can be particularly important for individuals who work in industries where their appearance is closely scrutinised, such as modelling or acting.

The appearance of cosmetic tattoos can also be customised to suit the individuals tastes and preferences. This customisation allows for a wide range of styles, from realistic depictions of the missing limb to more abstract designs. Some individuals may choose to incorporate meaningful symbols or imagery into their tattoos, while others may opt for a more decorative approach. By choosing their own designs and styles, individuals can take an active role in the healing process and make the tattoos a meaningful part of their journey.

It is important to note that cosmetic tattoos are not without drawbacks or risks, like any tattoo there is a risk of infection or allergic reaction. An individual should carefully consider their own health and the potential risks for undergoing the procedure. Additionally the tattoos are not guaranteed to last forever and may require touch-ups or maintenance over time. While risks may need to be considered, the potential benefits of cosmetic tattoos should not be overlooked or underestimated.

An aesthetically pleasing prosthetic limb can help amputees feel more comfortable and confident in their new bodies. The colour match, shape, size, material used, and socket fit, all play a crucial role in the overall appearance and must be carefully considered during the prosthetic creation and fitting process. As prosthetic technology continues to advance it is important to prioritise the cosmetic appearance of prosthetic limbs to help regain confidence and acceptance of their new physical being. This no doubt applies to the younger amputee more than the older one where body image and peer pressure is seen to be more important.

There are many things that contribute to a poor looking prosthesis. If it looks too bulky or coloured wrongly, this will make it highly visible to any onlookers. If straps, buckles, or buttons appear obvious through clothing, and is therefore not consistent with the normal anatomy, it will draw attention to it. I had this problem initially because of the high amputation where my right buttock did not match the other side. The prosthetist eventually added padding, covered by leather to improve the appearance, and balance me more when sitting down.

Uncovered pylons lack the required material bulk and shape to provide matching symmetry and shape of the missing limb. I intensely disliked my first pylon leg I was given. There was just a quadrant shaped rocker where the foot should have been. It looked awful, and for me served no purpose in transitioning to a prosthesis with a foot on. It did not aid in any way my walking ability. I was only seventeen years old and looks were important to me as a teenager. By wearing this it fully underlined to everyone I was disabled, and anyone looking would have probably questioned what the weird looking shape was where the foot should have been! It still makes me shudder to this day!

The prosthetic covers can assist in prosthesis acceptance, promote functional recovery, and have a positive effect. I still remember to this day how elated I was to get my first fully functional shaped prosthetic leg. Good cosmetic covers can serve an important role in the rehabilitation of those with lower limb amputation.

Body image may be particularly affected following amputation, including initial "preparatory" prosthesis delivery. Preparatory prostheses may contribute to disappointment like I was. This is because cosmetic covers are not routinely applied with preparatory prostheses, which is the limb provided to patients at a time when most are still coping with limb loss.

Prosthetic acceptance is influenced by comfort, function, and the covering used. Similarly, body image is influenced by social values including vitality, fitness, and physical appearance. Use of a cosmetically covered prosthesis may improve body image, self-acceptance, and social acceptance. This helps to provide a means of presenting oneself to others and allows the individual to be seen first, before potentially revealing a disability. I often have had people say to me they thought I had a slight hip problem for instance, which I strangely found comforting because it meant my disability did not show too much.

As a footnote to the cosmetic appearance of amputees, it is transitory, but what you do, the way you think is far more attractive. After all it is good to celebrate your being different and unique because true beauty resides within a good heart, not in superficial things like hair, makeup, clothes, or a nice looking artificial limb.

Jim - This subject has as many twists and turns, highs and lows, opinions, and variables as there are fish in the oceans. Your age and sex have everything to do with how you want to present yourself to the world. Younger people, including amputees spend more time on their appearance while older people tend to spend less time. Older amputees tend to go for comfort rather than fashion.

In my case, I have worn pants on one occasion in 5½ years and the rest of the time, shorts. I loved good-looking, fashionable ties and had a bunch of them. I kept one tie just to remember what they are! There was a time when you would not think about getting on a plane without a coat and tie or fancy dress. Today, it is flip flops and sweat suits. The entire world has gone casual.

Many amputees are more self-conscious because we do look 'different' than the general population. It is hard for me to relate to people who are obsessed with their appearance because I have never had any issues with living in my own skin. I am confident with who I am, and comfortable living as I am, as an amputee.

Increased numbers of people are wrapping their sockets/prosthesis with everything possible from pictures of flowers to sports team logos. I decided to wrap my latest socket in an Americana theme for a couple reasons. Firstly, plain black sockets are boring and depressing and secondly, it would grab attention, stimulate conversation, and cause assumptions and stereotypes in strangers who see it. My socket has a bold version of the American flag with a fierce looking American bald eagle emblazoned on it. When I am out in public, I make sure my socket shows. Eventually, someone passing will say, 'Thank You For Your Service.' I have not been in the military. I was planning to be a pilot and had an appointment to The United States Air Force Academy but, during my High School senior year, I dislocated my shoulder playing football and could not pass the physical. The passers-by saw my 'Flag Socket,' my buzz cut hair cut, my miliary demeanour and immediately assumed I was a veteran. We amputees need to have a little fun just to survive.

Chapter 23:

Ageing Gracefully

I believe whether you are an amputee or not, we all want to grow old gracefully. This is more about being healthy and happy than keeping grey hair or wrinkles at bay. To do this, there are several crucial aspects to address. There is the physical health, your mental health, and psychological well-being including environmental factors which include a healthy social life to consider.

I recently read some tips on ageing gracefully for every one of us, whether able-bodied or disabled. They include: -

- **Living in the Moment** – None of us knows what the future holds, the past is done, the future still to happen, so make the most of each moment and be aware every day of what you do. Treasure it because most look back remembering those special times rather than living them more fully as they happen.

- **Forgive Yourself and Others** – This is not an easy one to address and means you do not condone whatever occurred, but you do let go of the events which have a negative hold on your mind and body.

- **Find Humour and even Laugh at Yourself** – Look at the lighter side of life instead of dwelling on the darker elements. Laughing is a great tonic and we all feel better after a good, hearty laugh. As difficult as it can be at traumatic times, humour is a marvellous tonic. Laughter enhances your intake of oxygen-rich air, stimulates your heart, lungs, muscles, and increases the endorphins that are released by your brain. All of this activates and relieves your stress.

- **Stay Curious** – An active mind is healthy, and no-one is ever too old to learn something new. Even new hobbies or the ever developing world of social media is something to consider.

- **Be Flexible in Mind and Body** – There are several approaches which might be beneficial to movement, breathing and provide an improved mental outlook. These include Pilates, Yoga and Tai-Chi. I remember on a business trip I went to in China, when I looked out of the hotel window in Shanghai just as dawn was breaking to see a few people mulling about in a square. In the next ten minutes another fifty people suddenly appeared performing Tai-Chi. It was so peaceful, rhythmic, and graceful. I could see how rewarding it was for those participants who after about twenty minutes all seemed rejuvenated by it, smiling to each other as they continued their daily tasks. It did leave a lasting impression.

- **Meditation** – This comes in many forms and is not just closing your eyes to produce a deep state of relaxation in a tranquil mind. It can be through prayer, writing, gardening, fishing, or anything where time flies by because you are having fun and not focussing on stressful thoughts. This results in enhanced physical and emotional well-being.

- **Be Grateful** – Learn to appreciate the good things, and good people around you. We all take things for granted; it is a human trait after all, but stepping back to look at the effort by others gives an appreciation often forgotten. When I go for repairs on my prosthesis, I am often grateful for only having lost only one limb when I see others far worse off than me.

Maintaining physical health is crucial for an amputee's well-being and healthy eating, exercising, and maintaining a healthy weight are all vital components of this. It is important to stay active and maintain a healthy weight to reduce the risk of secondary complications like heart disease, hypertension, and diabetes. Exercising helps us all stay physically fit and boosts the mood. Just walking a short distance for me is good exercise because of the exertion involved.

To age gracefully amputees must also prioritise self-care, this includes regular skin monitoring, maintaining proper hygiene and dealing with phantom pains. Regular skin monitoring is necessary to avoid any pressure sores or skin infections, which can lead to severe and potentially life threatening complications. Maintaining proper hygiene also helps prevent any infections in the residual limb. The management of phantom pain is essential to help amputees remain pain free, and various medications are available to help manage this. Some medications are more successful than others, but being pain free for much of the time gives greater pleasure to life.

The loss of a limb can affect a person's mental health and psychological well-being. It can lead to depression, anxiety, and post-traumatic stress disorder. We are ageing from the day we are born but must all consider our mental health at times. It is important to seek support from friends and family members, perhaps attend counselling sessions and join support groups. These measures can help to address emotions and cope effectively with any challenges which arise.

Creating an environment that is supportive, safe, and accessible is essential. Amputees, as we know, must ensure their home and workplace are accessible and safe. This includes installing aids such as handrails, non-slip mats, grab rails and wheelchair ramps for ease of mobility. It is also important to adhere to daily routines and schedules which provides structure and help to maintain a sense of control over their lives.

It is important to prioritise your social life and engage in activities which bring pleasure. Staying socially active can help reduce loneliness and depression which boosts overall mental health. Joining social activities, which may include a social club, volunteering, or pursuing a hobby will all help.

As we get older, we find the aches and pain no longer disappear but stay. Then it is a question of what hurts most on your body. With ageing comes muscle waste, which is why it is so important to keep healthy with a slow, yet steady approach for older amputees. Small targets or milestones reached give a feeling of accomplishment and helps with motivation. We all have our comfort zones but pushing outside of it takes courage and commitment, sometimes even going through a pain barrier or two. It is easy to have a, 'Can't do' attitude but to keep pushing on through both mental and physical barriers will reap rewards.

Being so young when I lost my leg, I was still stronger and more agile than I am fifty plus years later. It is inevitable older amputees will not progress at the same rate a young amputee will. They may well have other health issues too and this can magnify the whole recovery program after amputation by having less reserve in the tank than when younger. No matter what medical conditions you may experience, appropriate daily exercise keeps you connected with the outside world and leads to a better quality of life.

Wearing a prosthesis is not natural and it does take a toll on your body. Changes in gait and posture redistribute the weight burden throughout the whole body, and repetitive activities can take a toll. If I walk on a good day, a few hundred yards, I get neck pain, which I know is directly related to the burden my prosthesis puts on my body and my whole body's misalignment. I learnt this long ago and recognise the beginning of associated problems arising.

It is quite surprising how little things upset the equilibrium of your body and moreso when wearing a prosthetic. For instance, I had a bad ache in my lower back which I thought was some misalignment of my prosthesis. It would not go away, and I made an appointment for getting a repair done. I discussed it with the prosthetist and between us we resolved the problem. He never even had to touch the prosthesis because the back pain was caused by me changing the shoes I wore. The heel on the new shoes were about half an inch (12mm) lower than my previous pair and this was what was causing my backache. When I got home, I changed shoes and within a day my back pain had gone. Simple dynamics but a real lesson for me about footwear. This is why the relationship with your prosthetist is so important because your quality of life rests in the dual understanding of working together.

It is important to embrace new technology, and this must be balanced with the benefits you will get. Every long term amputee will always have a favourite prosthesis and will be reluctant to change. Over the years when mine came to the end of its working life and was condemned, I thoroughly disliked changing to a new one. It would take several weeks for my body to adjust to it and invariably minor tweaks were needed at the Enablement Repair Centre. What I wear today is no longer being made and there are very few spare parts available for it and I dread the time to come when change is required.

I am not a complete dinosaur though and have embraced change. For instance, the more comfort you are going to have in the socket, the more activities you are going to be able to do, and the more stability you will eventually have. There are activity trackers like a FitBit or Apple Watch available, which incidentally I have bought for my wife, or even a smart phone can track you. These wearable activity monitoring devices allow for a person to track their daily activity whether it be at steps or heart rate, with real-time feedback to help with making progress and recognizing your goal achievement. These are a good indicator for amputees to track progress being made.

One of the changes I hoped to make was the wearing of a new innovative socket called a 'bikini style socket' which I discussed with my prosthetist. This new prosthetic was lighter, easier to put on and take off, but the biggest attraction to me was the potential to walk for longer periods in more comfort. It was designed in the USA for someone who had a hip disarticulation amputation three years before I tried it. I corresponded with someone who had this type of amputation and was starting to use it in Manchester, England with stunning results.

At my first fitting I was surprised at how minimal the socket was, which made it much lighter to wear. It was also a lot more comfortable to sit in than the conventional socket as you are not as enclosed, so sweating is lessened. The straps were ratchet buckles tightening over the hips rather than across the abdomen, so the control and gait are much improved. The leg itself was about two thirds of the weight of my existing artificial leg and the fitting around my waist was a ratchet system, different from the Velcro straps I had. It had to be pulled very tight into your body so there was no movement between your socket and the skin. My existing strap just went around my waist, but the new leg had straps or supports from the back of the leg over each hip which were ratcheted very tight. It was so tight I could hardly breathe and when I took my first few steps in the rails it was not the improvement I had expected. It felt unstable and I could not tighten it anymore.

For a few months we tried various ways to improve the leg to suit me but, in the end, I had to concede it just was not suitable for me. I believe it is a great improvement for those with hip disarticulation, but it is not suitable for those, like me, with a hemipelvectomy. Part of my right hip bone was removed in my amputation, and I do not have the same support someone with a hip disarticulation amputation has. I was quite disappointed because even one percent improvement would have been worth it but at least I had tried to embrace change, even in my late sixties.

With ageing, everybody experiences changes in balance and strength, but compensating can be especially problematic for amputees. I have noticed recently more difficulty when I am gardening because I invariably sit on the floor to do it, then get up, and move a short distance. It is this getting up, which never bothered me in the slightest but now seems to take more effort.

I can understand the trauma involved when losing a limb in later life especially for those just struggling with ageing, let alone an amputation. It is why safety is so important to avoid the compounded problems of falls. Being able to use a prosthesis for safer wheelchair transfers or household mobility may lessen the risk of these falls. It will also help increase the person's sense of independence and help with their sense of progress. Even standing can be a very significant task for some older amputees. I can therefore empathise with those not willing to persevere with a prosthetic, even if it limits the quality of life and their independence somewhat.

Nobody can escape the ravages of time, but we can embrace it positively. In terms of self-acceptance it relates to all your attributes which are embraced both positively and negatively. It is in effect a personal evaluation of your ageing and enables you to make choices which suit you. Staying active is important, but still recognising the impact an amputation can have on you physically. I cannot walk far at all, and my approach to fitness comes from doing gardening and understanding my diet. Food is one of life's pleasures, but this must be balanced by healthy food. The top causes of death for adults over the age of sixty five is heart disease. Using disease prevention strategies, such as eating a healthy diet, quitting smoking, and maintaining a healthy weight, can help to avoid or reduce the impact of some these conditions.

What I never want to do is just drift along as I age without any sense of purpose. Time travels fast enough as it is, without having no purpose. If you have a feeling of well-being and satisfaction with yourself and the world around you, then you are probably doing something meaningful and not just living to pass the time of day. By having friendships, or interaction with people of all ages. this helps reduce stereotyping and prejudice about different age groups. Social media for instance is a good place to have this interaction with so many groups on every subject available.

They say, 'You are never too old to learn', which is quite important as you age because learning can sharpen your mental health and slow the progression of decline. Lifelong learning can also help strengthen memory and recall skills. I remember the feeling of a cliff edge following retirement, having a lifetimes experience and being a subject matter expert was all suddenly gone, and would not be used again. It was a void to be filled and so many other things filled the space, followed by writing. We must all find our pathways to happiness whether able bodied or disabled to lead a happy, healthy, and fulfilled life. A recent sign stated, 'It's important to have a twinkle in your wrinkle'. Is that not food for thought?

Jim – *I have only been acquainted with John Paffett for a short while after he posted a request on a media site for an 'Ageing Senior' to make comments on each chapter of his book on ageing as it relates to them personally.*

I enjoy writing and have a mission to help amputees; especially to get through the first years of being an amputee. It soon became apparent that John and I share similar philosophies about life as an amputee. This chapter is a prime example of that. Since my amputation, I have become much more philosophical about living life as an amputee as well as life in general. To use an American football analogy - At my age, I am in the 'Red Zone' of life and can see crossing the goal line in the not-too-distant future.

I am in total agreement with the key points in this chapter, like living in the moment, forgive yourself and others, find humour, and laugh at yourself and all the other points outlined in the chapter.

I would like to address one of the other areas related to ageing gracefully and that is 'Your Legacy.' As amputees, we have a unique opportunity to influence the future for others who will become amputees. Your legacy is not just possessions or money. A legacy is an opportunity for you to change the world for good! Your legacy gives you an opportunity to live for a purpose which is bigger than yourself. No one leaves a legacy by accident. In my view, you must live life on purpose and develop a plan to help other amputees and advocate to others in positions of influence who can provide the resources to meet the needs of you and your fellow amputees.

Here are three keys to creating your 'lasting legacy':

1. Pass along your values. Become a leader other amputees can depend on for support by sharing your experience to help them overcome their challenges. Help the non-amputee sector understand the unique challenges amputees face. Be visible and vocal.

2. Practice outrageous generosity. We are not talking about money. If you want to multiply your legacy's impact and have fun while you are at it, develop a plan to share your time, knowledge, and experience to help other amputees. Giving will inspire joy like nothing else! It is the antidote for selfishness and one of the greatest secrets of a meaningful legacy.

3. Have a plan to transition your legacy. Instil your legacy in others so the momentum you created will carry forward and continue to grow to help future amputees. Unfortunately, the projected number of amputees will increase at an alarming rate. With all of us amputees working together to educate people, it may help stem the tide. That will be our legacy.

Chapter 24:

Amputee Humour

I personally believe one of life's greatest gift's is a sense of humour. It has helped me enormously over the years throughout my life's journey. Not just because I am an amputee but in appreciation of what a hearty laugh does for you in raising your spirits and bringing a smile to your face and others.

Many amputees turn to humour to help maintain a positive attitude and cope with their disability. Along with the most important benefits of humour, is its ability to reduce stress, and anxiety. Laughter is a powerful antidote to stress, and it can help you to reduce the levels within the body. By reducing stress and anxiety, humour can help you feel more relaxed and comfortable in social situations, which can be particularly important if you are self-conscious about your disability.

Another benefit of humour is it can help to relieve pain. Studies have shown that laughter releases endorphins, the body's natural painkillers, which can help to reduce pain levels. For the many of us who experience phantom limb pain, humour can be a welcome distraction from the discomfort.

It can also help to build social connections and reduce feelings of isolation. When amputees can joke about their disability with others, it can help to break down barriers and create a sense of camaraderie. It can also help to educate others about their disability and promote acceptance and understanding. Moreover humour can be a powerful coping mechanism for dealing with negative emotions like grief and depression. By finding humour in this situation amputees can create a positive mindset and shift their focus away from negative thoughts and feelings. They can also help to foster resilience and a sense of control over their situation. In some cases humour can even help to find meaning in their disability and use their experience to help others.

It is essential to remember not all amputees find humour helpful or appropriate. Some may not even have a sense of humour, and some might find it offensive, insensitive and a trivialising of their experiences. It is important to respect each other's individual preferences and to ensure humour is used in a respectful and appropriate manner. Humour is not a cure for the challenges of living with limb loss, but it can be a valuable tool for maintaining a positive outlook and promoting emotional well-being.

Amputation can lead to various negative emotions such as sadness, anger, frustration, and anxiety. Coping with these emotions can be challenging and many amputees use different strategies to deal with them. Humour is one such strategy that many use as a positive escape to deal with the challenges that come with their disability. Humour is a distraction and helps to focus on positive aspects of life, allowing them to temporarily forget about their disability related issues. This distraction can help to feel less anxious or stressed, thereby promoting better mental health, thereby viewing their disability in a better light. This positive outlook can provide amputees with the resilience they might need to face the challenges of everyday life by forging a positive attitude.

Humour helps to breakdown social barriers, and it is often used to break ice in social situations by building connections with others. By making light of their disability, amputees can create an atmosphere of acceptance and understanding, promoting inclusivity. It also helps to develop a sense of control over their lives, by finding humour in their situation they can feel empowered and use their experience to inspire and educate others. It can also help to feel less self-conscious about their disability by promoting greater self-confidence.

It must be remembered that humour is not a panacea and should not be used to ignore or deny the challenges of limb loss. It is essential to acknowledge everyone's experiences are unique, and humour may not be an appropriate mechanism for everyone. Additionally humour should never be used as an excuse to make fun of someone's disability or discriminate against them. It can only be reiterated that humour can be an essential tool for promoting greater mental health and well-being amongst amputees, provided it is approached with sensitivity and respect.

There is another side to humour which is self-deprecating humour and can be a great way for amputees to cope with their disability. This type of humour is used to diffuse awkwardness, east tension, and make light of what can be a difficult situation, I have reservations about it, but for some it works. Sometimes for me lines are crossed, and the humour stops. By poking fun at themselves, they can take control of their situation and promote a more positive outlook. There are many comedians nowadays on the modern circuit who are disabled and talk openly about their disability and laugh with the audience. Again it must be remembered, humour which belittles or demeans disabled individuals can be hurtful and harmful.

This type of humour can be controversial and offensive to some individuals, but it can also be used to assert control over a disability and show they are not defined by it. Another reason self-deprecating humour is used is to challenge societies norms and stereotypes surrounding disabilities. Often, individuals with disabilities are viewed as weak, helpless, or dependent. By using humour to poke fun at themselves they can challenge these stereotypes and show they are capable of being confident, independent, and humorous. Self-deprecating humour can therefore be a healthy way to cope and can help amputees feel more comfortable with themselves and others.

Amputees might make a joke about always being one step ahead because they have only one leg or refer to their prosthetic limb as their bionic leg. I have a grandson who refers to me as 'robo-grandad', as an example, which is fine by me. He is always wanting to see my prostheses and I accept this curiosity which is a natural childlike need. I do not have a problem with it, they find it amusing, so it is win-win and encourages disability awareness.

On the other side of the coin, some individuals with disabilities may find it inappropriate to make fun of themselves in a way that others may not be able to relate to. I remember years ago playing darts in a pub for a team I belonged to. When it came to my turn, someone said quite openly for all to hear, 'You should win this as you are playing a cripple'. A thoughtless, hurtful, cruel, and upsetting thing to say, but then it was a sign of the times, fifty years ago, reflecting some of the stigma society had for disabilities all those years ago. We have come a long way forward since then, thank goodness.

Another great way to incorporate humour without being insensitive is to use sarcasm, irony, or satire. For example instead of using humour that mocks the physical challenges of living with limb loss, they could joke about the societal challenges they face. They could make a joke about how they are now part of the disabled parking mafia war or how they can get away with anything by simply blaming it on their disability. Irony and satire can be used to highlight the absurdity of some of the challenges amputees face in a way that is non-offensive and enjoyable.

This type of humour is often used to bring attention to the struggles of amputees and to challenge the ableist stereotypes which exist in society. Irony and satire are used to create a sense of exaggeration, absurdity, or silliness about the realities of living with an amputation. Satire is often used to criticise societal attitudes towards disability, like poking fun at the widespread belief that people with disabilities are always in need of pity or assistance.

Humour which is educational can be a great way to raise awareness and promote inclusivity. Jokes which highlight the experiences of amputees can help to educate people about the unique challenges they face while also helping them to feel accepted and understood. For instance they might joke about having to constantly explain their situation to others or how they always must be the centre of attention because of their disability. These types of jokes could be used to create a sense of community and promote greater understanding of limb loss.

Educational humour is a form which aims to educate people about the experiences of individuals who have undergone amputations. This can be used to break down barriers and misconception about disability and promote awareness and understanding of the challenges faced by individuals. It can take many forms, for instance it could be used to explain the functioning of prosthetic limbs to non-amputees. By joking about the various adjustments and maintenance required for prosthetic limbs they may be able to make the experience more accessible and understandable to others. This type of humour could therefore be used to explain the physical and emotional difficulties faced in everyday life, such as phantom pains, and the loss of mobility and independence.

Humour is a powerful tool, and it can also be used to encourage people to take a more proactive role in supporting individuals with disabilities. For example they might use humour to encourage people to speak up against discrimination, to advocate for policies that ensure equal access and opportunities for individuals with disabilities. By using humour they make these issues more palatable and engaging which can encourage people to become more involved in the cause of disability rights.

This type of humour can also be used to provide context and perspective on the broader issues surrounding disability. We can highlight the ways in which society's attitudes towards disability can be harmful and limiting, demonstrating the importance of challenging these attitudes. It can demonstrate the value of diversity and how amputees and individuals with disabilities can make unique contributions to society.

Again it is important to note educational humour should always be used in a sensitive and respectful manner. They should always be mindful of the potential for their humour to offend or alienate others and strive to create humour which is both informative and non-threatening. They should be used to promote understanding and acceptance not to belittle, stereotype or mock individuals with disabilities thus causing exclusion and division.

Humour can be used to celebrate the resilience and strength of amputees, for example they might create a humorous skit or performance which highlights their accomplishments and the ways in which they have overcome their disability. This type of humour is a great way to promote self-confidence and inspire others to live their best lives no matter what challenges they face. It also focuses on the positive aspects of amputee experiences such as their resilience and strength in the face of adversity. It is often used to inspire and motivate others, and to celebrate the accomplishments and success of individuals who have undergone amputations.

One of the ways this type of humour is used is to emphasise the sheer determination and persistence that is required to overcome the challenges of amputation. They might joke about the long and difficult road to recovery, highlighting the humour in the absurdity of the process. This can inspire others to adopt similar mindsets with perseverance and determination which can provide hope they too can overcome similar challenges.

Another way used is to highlight the successes and accomplishments of individuals who have undergone amputations in achieving longstanding goals or accomplishments. The Paralympics is an example to all of what can be achieved by a few dedicated souls inspired through adversity. This type of humour can inspire others to strive towards their own goals and dreams and to see amputees as role models of strength and resilience.

Humour can be used to challenge negative stereotypes and biases about individuals without amputations by celebrating their strength and resilience. It can show they are not defined by their disability, that they are capable, accomplished individuals who can contribute to society in meaningful ways. This could help to break down barriers and promote greater acceptance and inclusion of individuals with disabilities. Humour should be used to uplift and inspire, never to shame or ridicule. It is important to be sensitive to the feelings and experiences of others and to use humour in a respectful and thoughtful manner rather than to hurt or ostracise.

Amputee humour can be very powerful and meaningful, but it is necessary to recognise it can also cross the line and be inappropriate or offensive. Sometimes it can unwittingly be hurtful to the individuals it is meant to celebrate, as well as to others who may be struggling with their disability. There are several reasons why this humour may not be funny and why it is important to be mindful of the potential harm because this can lead to further marginalisation and exclusion of amputees in society. For example jokes about amputee's being helpless or dependant on others can perpetuate the idea that individuals with disabilities are burdensome or incapable. This not only diminishes the value of amputee experiences but also reinforces harmful stereotypes about disability. It is a fine line at times!

Secondly amputee humour can be hurtful to individuals who may be struggling with amputations or disabilities. Even if the humour is not intended to be malicious, it can still be insensitive and distressing to those who are dealing with the physical and emotional challenges. Jokes about prosthetics, phantom pain or mobility issues can trivialise the difficult experiences some individuals with amputations face and cause unnecessary pain and discomfort.

Finally it can also be hurtful to friends, family and colleagues of amputees who may not understand the humour or who may find it inappropriate or offensive. This can result in strained relationships and feelings of isolation for the amputee who may feel misunderstood or unsupported by those around them. It should also be remembered not everyone has a sense of humour and would not necessarily understand the content or context to laugh at it.

I remember just three weeks after my amputation when my Dad was visiting me in hospital. There was always a concern the cancer would return, and I made a joke with him. I said I had five lumps appearing, just near the scar line of the amputation, and I could see his stricken face at the thought of the cancer reoccurring with all the implications of it. I then said, 'I think it is my toes starting to grow back'. I really laughed but he did not see the funny side of it. We had different humour. I thought it funny, and he did not, and now looking back after what he, as a parent, had been going through it must have been real gallows humour. We should always be aware of our audience and the sensitivities involved.

Humour is a personal thing and what is funny to one person is not to another. I have read and seen on tee-shirts some very funny things and others I found distasteful. In reading some of the jokes below I hope they bring a smile, but if not then groan and please forgive me.

Tee-shirt printed jokes:

- **You can count on me, but only up to 15.**

- **It's official. I am on my last leg.**

- **Personality 9/10**
  Looks 8/10

- **Before you ask it was a shark.**

Verbal Jokes:

- **It takes a pretty twisted person to mock an amputee. Honestly, just try putting yourself in their shoe.**

- **Why don't foot amputees really care when they lose a game? Because they are used to being defeated.**

- **Did you hear about the amputee who nearly died from an allergic reaction? Apparently, he was lack-toes intolerant.**

- **My amputee buddy asked me for a hand. I didn't believe he had the nerve to say that.**

No more jokes now because most I have heard before. When people tell me a joke, I must smile and let them think it is the first time anyone has said it. I am sure most long-term amputees will tell you the same thing.

The impact of distasteful jokes should not be underestimated, and it can last a lifetime. For someone who has lost a limb, hearing jokes about their situation can be hurtful and insensitive. Such jokes can be seen as trivialising the struggles and hardships they must overcome. It is important to remember people who have lost limbs are people, not punch lines. Not everyone is at the same level of comfort with disability and bodily differences. It is always important to consider the feelings of those who may be affected by amputee humour and make sure everyone is comfortable with the jokes being made. If in doubt, then do not say it. By respecting individuals and their experiences we can create a more inclusive and respectful world.

Jim - In "The States", we spell 'Humour – Humor!! This is my favourite chapter in the book because I feel so strongly about keeping as much humour in your life as possible, regardless of your physical situation, amputee or not. It is the great pressure relief valve and in today's world, we certainly need more humour in our lives. It is 'The Great Diffuser'.

John covers the various aspects of humour as it is perceived differently by people. One person's joke is another person's insult. Being the positive person I am, I never give much thought to how something I think is funny could be interpreted as not funny. Granted, there are obvious off-colour, rude, and unacceptable jokes and stories, but I find them to be limited and just add the person telling it to my 'Jerk" list.

'He has a great sense of humour' or 'He has no sense of humour.' What exactly is a 'Sense of humour?' I find there is a great correlation between a person's personality and the degree of sense of humour they possess. By my unscientific observation, people that have more positive and outgoing personalities seem to have a higher degree of humour sense. I believe we consciously and unconsciously decide what our personality is going to become. I choose to be positive and outgoing. As amputees we can decide what our personality will be after amputation. I choose to try to be the person who people say, 'That Jimbo, he has a great sense of humour.' I work on my personality and sense of humour which gives me the ability to say funny things and to see the funny side of things. Nothing makes me feel better than putting a smile on someone's face and causing them to laugh a little. I get the feeling it just makes their day a little brighter.

The supermarket is my stage and laboratory. I use an electric shopping cart and purposely ask people to help me get things I cannot reach. Then I say, 'You get the Atta Girl, or Guy Award, or a Gold Star', and wait for the reaction. I get direct and immediate insight into the persons personality and sense of humour. Some smile and/or make a come-back comment to a deadpan stare and no comment. I immediately know which one I want to associate with. From one end of the positive spectrum to the other negative end. Try it sometime!

Heard this one? 'Laughter is the best medicine.' It is true! A healthy sense of humour can help you deal with tough times. Humour might seem like a soothing balm or a light diversion, but humour is much more powerful than something which simply lulls us or calms us down.

In fact, it is an often-overlooked tool in our arsenal in the battle to maintain good health. During times when we are barraged with economic, social, political, and health problems, it is wise to turn to a not-so-obvious way to protect ourselves. The myriad of health benefits of humour and laughter are wide-reaching.

During moments of levity, while it seems like you are simply laughing at a friend's joke or a comedian's monologue, you are improving your health. By tickling your funny bone, clinical evidence shows you are not only being entertained but enhancing your physical, psychological, and social well-being.

Humour is a great way to improve your health and well-being. According to various studies, humour can have many benefits for your physical, mental, and social health. Some of these benefits are:

• Humour can stimulate your organs, such as your heart, lungs, and muscles, by increasing your oxygen intake and releasing endorphins.

• Humour can relieve stress and tension by activating your stress response and then cooling it down, resulting in a relaxed feeling

• Humour can boost your immune system by reducing negative thoughts and emotions that can weaken your immunity and increase the production of neuropeptides that fight stress and illness.

• Humour can ease pain by triggering the release of natural painkillers in your body.

• Humour can improve your mood by reducing anxiety and depression and increasing happiness and optimism.

• Humour can enhance your social skills by helping you connect with others, build rapport, diffuse conflicts, and cope with challenges.

As you can see, humour has many positive effects on your health and wellbeing. To enjoy these benefits, you can try to add more humour to your life by doing things that make you laugh, such as watching funny shows, reading jokes, or spending time with humorous people. You can also develop your sense of humour by being more playful, spontaneous, and creative in your daily life. Humour is a natural and powerful way to heal yourself and others. So do not forget to laugh often and have fun!

Doctors and mental health professionals cite plenty of research to remind us that laughter contributes to positive health outcomes. Laughter has been shown in studies to improve your pain threshold, due to an endorphin mediated opiate effect. What is interesting is this appears to be independent of your mood, meaning it can have a positive effect even when you are down. Proven processes are working behind the scenes in your body to increase your pain tolerance. Endorphins, for example, get to work. Because you're laughing up a storm, your body produces these natural painkillers.

Switching gears, I would like to discuss the impact modern communication has had on amputee humour and the amputee world in general. Back in the day, jokes and other humorous materials were circulated by word of mouth and some printed material. Then, along came burlesque, radio shows, TV, comedy clubs, college tours, records, and other outlets, then the six headed monster appeared, the internet. A person can put an amputee joke on YouTube and within seconds, millions of people around the world can see and hear it. It can have a tremendous impact, either positive or negative.

Using a search engine, if you type in "Amputee humour", you will get about 1,170,000 results in 0.35 seconds. How are you going to react to this bombardment of unrelenting exposure? Over a million titbits of information in one-third of a second! Mind Boggling!

Looking on the bright side, we can use this powerful tool to benefit and promote the welfare of amputees worldwide. Estimates suggest there may be as many as one hundred million amputees living worldwide. There are over one million new limb amputations globally every year, one every thirty seconds. Just over two million people in the United States are living with limb loss, and that number is expected to double by 2050. Currently, just under two hundred thousand amputations are performed annually in the United States.

This side story is related to finding humour and laughing at yourself. I recently attended my first class on learning to perform 'Stand Up Comedy', even though I cannot stand up exceptionally long. I am going to develop a gig about life as an amputee. We live in a 55+ community. One of the residents is a retired professional comedian and has agreed to conduct six, one-hour classes on how to become a 'Stand-Up Comedian'. I signed up but I will probably not qualify to participate because I cannot

stand up! I am going to create a whole new classification of comedians –
'Sit Down Comedians'!

Chapter 25:

The Strong Amputee

Traditionally the term strong is used to describe someone with superior physical strength, however, in modern times the term has taken on a new meaning with one which encompasses not only physical strength but also emotional and mental strength.

Amputees are individuals who have experienced the loss of a limb due to a medical condition or traumatic injury and losing a limb can be a life changing event which can have physical and emotional consequences. However, with our enduring human spirit, amputees can be strong both physically and mentally, learning to adapt to their new circumstances, push the limits and live a fulfilling life, despite their challenges.

One of the defining characteristics of the strong amputee is physical strength. Losing a limb does not mean losing the ability to be physically active. I recently watched a short film clip of someone who had lost most of his leg and yet was doing weightlifting. He had a superbly honed body and was amazing. Many engage in sports and other physical activities such as, hiking, skiing, and even surfing. With the use of prosthetic limbs and adaptive equipment they can perform at high level, and in some cases even outperform their able bodied counterparts. You only need to watch the Paralympics and see the examples of what can be achieved, despite having a disability.

Physical strength is not limited to sports. Many have physically demanding jobs, such as construction workers, firefighters, and police officers. They perform their duties with the same level of dedication and strength as their able bodied colleagues. A few years back when I was having my prosthesis repaired at the Enablement Centre, a marine sergeant appeared with his beret on, in full fatigues. He had a below knee amputation and was having a titanium leg made because the normal material used could not take the stresses and strains, he was putting it through. He then said he would appreciate it if his leg could be finished quickly as he had a twenty mile yomp with a heavy backpack to do. Wow!

Losing a limb can be a profound traumatic loss and that can take its toll on a person's emotional well-being. It not only affects the individual, but the family on all levels. How each of us choose to deal with their amputation will help determine the quality of life ahead. However strong amputees do have the emotional strength to overcome their challenges and live a fulfilling life. They learn to accept the new reality, cope with their emotions, and find meaning in their experiences.

One of the most significant strengths is the ability to adapt to their environment. Losing a limb can significantly affect an individual's daily activities but us humans are known for our creative problem solving skills to overcome these limitations. We learn to navigate the world in new ways, using assistive devices such as prosthetics, wheelchairs, or crutches and are often very resourceful in finding solutions which work.

Amputees also display tremendous resilience in the face of adversity. Those who have undergone amputation must cope with physical pain, phantom limb sensations, and emotional trauma. However we continue to persevere and stay positive even when faced with significant challenges. A challenge I recently read about was a double above-knee amputee aiming to be the first to climb Mount Everest. I wish him well.

Dealing with limb loss can take a toll on an individual's mental health. Some may experience feelings of depression, anxiety, or lack of self-confidence; however one way is work hard to maintain a positive attitude, and a sense of humour, even in the face of adversity. Many seek out mental health services to help them cope with their emotions and some even use their experiences to inspire others who may be going through similar challenges. Some are motivational speakers around the world. It is a global fraternity.

In this fraternity there is strength found, including with disability advocates. They share their experiences, offering support to one another and advocate for increased access ability, resources, and rights. Many also serve as role models and mentors to others helping them to navigate the difficulties of limb loss and find their own strength through this.

One of the essential elements of emotional strength is resilience. Those who are resilient learn to bounce back from adversity and thrive in the face of challenges. They have a positive attitude, a strong sense of purpose, and a supportive network of family and friends. Not everyone is like this though. A recent amputee, suddenly being dependent and feeling a loss of control over their lives, is one of the most frustrating changes people experience after amputation. It is important to recognize what you can control and what things are beyond your control. Regaining control over your life can begin in small ways and is the start of being strong.

One of the defining characteristics of emotionally strong amputees is acceptance. They have come to terms with their situation and understand their amputation does not define them. They recognise their disability is part of who they are but does not limit their potential.

Another critical element of emotional strength is self-love. Strong amputees have learnt to love and appreciate themselves for who they are. They recognise their value is not based on their physical appearance, but on their character, talents, and contributions to society. They are resilient individuals who can bounce back from adversity. They have a positive attitude and are committed to their personal growth and development. They understand life is a journey which comes with its ups and downs. They are determined to overcome their challenges and thrive in their 'new', normal way.

Having a supportive network of family and friends is essential because they have people in their lives who encourage, lift, and inspire them. They can rely on their support system for emotional and practical support. They also find meaning in their experiences and understand their amputation is not a punishment but an opportunity to grow and learn. They use their experience to inspire and help others who are going through similar challenges, and in this way, it can help them. I have always found it better to give than receive.

Taking control of decision making as soon as possible is a positive thing to do. Family may have had to make decisions for you while you were ill but there comes a time when you can do this. Be clear with yourself and others as to what you can do for yourself, and how they can help if need be. Always remembering the family have your best interests at heart. Recognise your frustration at being dependent on others will lessen as you regain your independence and feel more comfortable only asking for help when needed. This too is a sign of strength and empowerment.

For some, taking care of your spiritual needs is a way of connecting with your inner self. Spirituality provides a deep connection to something bigger than your everyday life. Spirituality can be developed through religion, meditation, music, nature, being with other people and having hopes and dreams. Spirituality helps people recognize their physical appearance is but a small part of who they really are.

Letting go of the past and the way things used to be, can help change your focus to the possibilities of the here and now, and the future. This will help your resilience to everyday challenges. Living in the here and now will help you accept what has changed and can help you make the most of your life today. I do believe this to be so important yet for some so difficult.

In the forty nine years I worked, I hardly ever experienced anything which made me aware or uncomfortable about my disability from others I worked with. I always had a positive attitude and would always engage with them talking about my disability if asked. People generally interacted around me with the same level of comfort you have with yourself.

People say what really helps in the long term is to find positive meaning and purpose after their amputation. I have always felt it was and is devastating physically, but there is far more than this to consider. I have grown in humanity. I appreciate other people's situations far more, and particularly look at the helpers we often depend on, acknowledging their contribution to our new life and being part of the journey I am now on. I have experienced so many things I would otherwise never have seen or felt, and of course met so many kindred spirits too. I am a stronger person through my experiences where the sum of the parts is greater than the whole.

Another critical element to emotional strength is self-acceptance. Those who have accepted their situation and learned to love and appreciate themselves for who they are can overcome their emotional challenges and find the strength to move forward. No matter what life throws at us we all have the strength within us to overcome our challenges.

Over the years I have had many people say to me they would never be able to cope with life the way I have. My response is always the same because until something traumatic happens, none of us knows what inner strengths we are blessed with. We are all unique and of differing characters. Life is always challenging with choices to make every day. Inside we know what the right thing to do is in making the choices, but being human we sometimes make mistakes. It was after all Einstein who said, 'Anyone who has never made a mistake has never tried anything new.'

If we are growing as a person, the right choices become easier and more natural because with this comes inner peace. The more you do this, the stronger you become, and remember, what you get by achieving your goals is not as important as what you become by achieving your goals. Enjoy your journey.

Jim - Being an amputee requires quite a few 'Strong's'. They include being strong physically, mentally, spiritually, attitudinally, socially, psychologically, emotionally and have all of that bundled up in a package of self-motivation. While caregivers and supporters can provide a certain amount of motivation, if you are going to move forward with your life in a positive manner it is only going to happen if you are self-motivated to do so. No one can do it for you but yourself. Like the old cliché', 'If it is to be, it is up to me'. That about sums it up.

All of those '-allys' are not static. The dynamics of mood swings with good days and bad days are constantly changing them. It is hard to be 'On' 100% every day. The point is to be aware of areas where you are on a slippery slope from time to time and act or find help from others to take corrective steps and get the ship back on course.

Frequently, the loss of a limb is compared to the loss of a loved one. In those situations, The five stages of grief may come into the picture. They are denial, anger, bargaining, depression, and acceptance. Much has been written on this subject with more information on the internet. If you find yourself stuck in any of these areas, you might want to seek professional help.

Throughout, the course of this interesting project, I keep asking myself, 'Am I that different than those people we have been discussing who are dealing with all these problems and issues and are having trouble adjusting and moving forward?' After reading everything written, and reviewing everything I have written, I have concluded I am different from many amputees because many of these issues have not been a lingering problem for me. If an issue comes up, I deal with it and try to fix it. If I cannot fix it or get help to fix it, I kick it to the side of the road and move on.

I might be kidding myself, but I do not think I am that different with all those '-ally's' after my amputation than I was before amputation. Did I need to adjust in my daily life? Sure did, but I enjoyed using my brain to figure out how to do things creatively, from getting dressed to driving a car and everything in between, even if it takes me two or three times longer. It is fun figuring things out and I get a great sense of accomplishment from just a myriad of little things.

I think my positive attitude comes from playing football. Our team was undefeated for my three years on the team through high school. We had a fabulous coach who instilled the spirit of how to motivate ourselves to play for each other. We were responsible for our own actions for the benefit of each other and the team results. This attitude has stuck with me for my entire life regardless of where life has taken me.

This project has raised my awareness to be more compassionate in understanding other amputees needs and issues and helping them deal with life as an amputee to achieve a peace of mind we all deserve. Thank you, John.

Chapter 26:

Reflections

Ageing is a wonderful leveller of your thoughts on what is important in life. If the purpose of life is to evolve by learning and growing, then having an amputation, which was devastating physically, made me appreciate the experience of learning from this. I am sure I have evolved personally into a better, caring person through mine. I have learned to manage my expectations, limitations, emotions, and frustrations, far better for instance than if I was able bodied.

Being reflective transforms your thoughts into learning about how beliefs and values affect your happiness, life choices and goal achievements. Understanding how your beliefs and values affect you is the first step along this path. After all the purpose of life is to live it and experience what you can to the utmost while searching for newer and richer experiences. This does not have to be just physically because many experiences can be emotional too. For me when I listen to certain music, I can get transformed to a special place which is so wonderful it fills me with beauty and happiness, even making the hairs on my neck stand up. A quote I read stated, 'Music gives a soul to the universe, wings to the mind, flight to the imagination, and life to everything.' I guess that covers it!

Reflection is a deeper form of learning which allows us to retain every aspect of any experience, be it personal or professional. I remember the profound happiness I experienced a week after my amputation in Westminster Hospital in London when I was pushed in a wheelchair through the gardens. The birdsongs, the colours and smell of the flowers were all there before, but I never opened my eyes enough to see and experience them. There are none so blind as those that see. Everything was so vibrant and pleasurable. The veil was lifted that day and I have always remembered it. Nowadays the modern in vogue name is mindfulness, which is the practice of purposely bringing one's attention to the present-moment experience without evaluation. I did not need to evaluate it because all my senses were heightened to it. A real life lesson.

It was later I questioned myself why something took place then, and did I understand it. What the impact was, asking myself whether it should or would happen again, as opposed to just remembering it happened. I enjoyed the experience so much I have tried all my life, to step back at times when having one of these moments, to savour and immerse myself in it rather than look back and reflect on the experience afterwards.

When we use self-reflections, we gain a better understanding of ourselves, our motivations, and our behaviours. I expect most amputees self-reflect on their life when able-bodied because it is the normal response to the loss. It is the acceptance of the current situation and the coming to terms which can be difficult for some and may cause distress.

One of the biggest challenges which comes with pre-op amputation is emotional distress. Many have lived with their limbs for a long time and have become accustomed to them. Losing a limb can cause great emotional trauma, reflecting on a sense of loss, grief, and anger. It can lead to a sense of helplessness, depression, and anxiety, which can affect the persons overall sense of well-being. These issues need to be addressed with compassion and empathy to help and support them cope with the loss.

Reflecting on another challenge is the physical impact of the procedure. Amputation requires adaption to a completely new way of movement and lifestyle. They must relearn basic tasks, such as eating, dressing, and bathing. They also need rehabilitation and therapy to learn how to use prosthetics or wheelchairs, which can be time consuming and physically demanding. They often require long term physical and occupational therapy to help them regain their independence and improve their overall functionality.

There are also financial implications to consider if they do not come under the National Health Service in the UK. The cost of amputation surgery, rehabilitation and prosthetics can be expensive, and most may not have adequate financial resources to cover these expenses. This financial burden can add to the emotional distress of the patient and their family members, making it essential for healthcare and social workers to provide adequate resources and support throughout the whole process.

Managing post complications is another challenge which healthcare workers face when caring for the elderly undergoing pre-op amputations. Complications such as wound infection, poor wound healing, and phantom limb pain can all occur requiring careful monitoring and management. It is important to work closely with them to manage their pain, monitor their wound healing, and provide psychological support as needed.

Being an amputee is a life changing experience that can cause a range of emotions from grief, and anger through to resilience and acceptance. It is a complex and multifaceted experiences filled with both challenges and opportunities for growth. As an amputee, one must learn to adapt to a new way of life, which can be a challenging process. It can also be an opportunity for self-reflection when looking on the positive side of life.

One of the most difficult aspects of being in amputee is the loss of a limb or limbs. It is important to acknowledge the feelings of grief and anger and allow yourself time to grieve while also recognising it is possible to move forward and find new ways to live.

Being an amputee can be a defining part of one's identity, while it is not the only aspect of who someone is, it can shape their experiences and perspectives on the world. For some, this can result in a greater sense of empathy and understanding toward others who may be facing challenges. Despite the challenges which come with amputation there is also a sense of resilience and strength that emerges. Learning to adapt and overcome obstacles can be empowering and build confidence by creating a sense of community with others who have gone through similar experiences. I would add it is important to not just look outward. Look inward and truly examine your feelings and reasons which are troubling you or niggling away at you. I have done this, and it was not easy, but it was cathartic, almost liberating to recognise within you some of the reasoning behind your thought processes and actions.

Our society is changing as the population is ageing because of the dramatic advances made in the prevention, care, and management of disease. Before the discovery of insulin, it is doubtful that many diabetics would have lived long enough to develop gangrene of a lower extremity. Countless numbers of people are now reaching the age of sixty five or older with medical conditions which, fifty years ago, would have been fatal at a much earlier age. It is essential for future planning because this trend will continue as new medicines and gene therapy ensure we all live longer, but this will come at a cost.

As civilisation ages we like to think we are a caring society in which we treat all people with equal dignity and respect. We also look after its people and do not exclude anyone by ensuring access to basic goods and services to place them on an equal footing with others. The cost of caring is rising as we use more sophisticated equipment and medicines. Inequality is rising, with the poor getting poorer, and the rich getting richer. If we are to treat all people with equal respect and dignity there is much to improve, and it will take years to even move a little forward in this respect.

The top 1% in the world now own more wealth than the bottom 92%, and the fifty wealthiest Americans own more wealth than the bottom half of American society, some 165 million people. Poverty has become a death sentence, with those on lower incomes dying fifteen years earlier than the wealthy. I recently read, the two richest people in America, Jeff Bezos, and Elon Musk, now own more wealth than the bottom 40% of Americans combined. I will end up down a long and winding discussion of where democracy ends, because it is finite and then on the flip side the authoritarian rise of communism in its many forms is concerning. I will stop here!

I was an amputee before I first married, but for others it happens after the relationship has started. We are all different in terms of commitment to a relationship and some cannot accept the lifestyle change in a relationship when amputation happens. It is after all a life altering event which can bring significant changes to a person's physical and emotional well-being. The amputation affects not only the individual but also a partner or spouse and the dynamics of their relationship. It can test any relationship, but love endures.

When we enter a partnership with someone whether formally or informally there is a commitment to love and look after that someone. Love is a commitment and not just an emotion or feeling. You cannot separate love and commitment because they are one in the same. When you truly love someone, you are committing yourself to that individual through the hardships all relationships go through. Some of these hardships are challenging but working them through together can be rewarding and enrich the relationship. It is after all being consistent in attention, devotion, loyalty and showing you are willing to sacrifice. To me love is the essence of life.

Losing a limb can bring about feelings of grief, anger, frustration, and sadness as well as anxiety about the future. It is crucial for both to acknowledge and address these emotions whether through therapy, support groups, or open communication with each other. It is also important to be aware of their own emotions and how they may affect their ability to support their partner.

The other factor to consider is the physical impact of amputation. This can include changes in mobility, the need for assisting devices or prosthetics, and the impact on daily activities such as household chores, work, and hobbies. It is important for both to be aware of these changes and to adapt accordingly. This may involve making modifications to the home environment or seeking out resources and support groups to help navigate these changes.

Communication is vital in any relationship, but it becomes even more essential after amputation. It is important for both partners to have open and honest discussions about their feelings, concerns, and needs. This includes discussing any changes in physical intimacy and exploring new ways to maintain intimacy and connection within the relationship. It can be a difficult time which both have to contribute to, on the flip side it can be fun too.

Support is also key in coping, and this can come from family, friends support groups and healthcare professionals. It is important to have access to resources and support systems that can help navigate the physical and emotional challenges ahead.

What can be an extremely difficult time is if the relationship is not a strong one which can weather the stormy waters ahead, especially at a time when emotions for both are raw. This is when understanding and an empathic approach will help ease the trauma when each consider the others situation and needs.

After losing my first wife through cancer I realised it was important to find someone who is accepting and understanding of my situation. This meant finding someone who was willing to listen and empathise with the struggles which come with losing a limb. It also meant finding someone who was patient and willing to adapt to certain needs, whether that meant helping with daily tasks or providing emotional support. All this is something you learn about over time and not discuss at the first meeting, or you would not see them for dust! There are so many positives to talk about but there are underlying needs to understand and have a meaningful relationship. For this reason, and because it was the second time around, and we both had children, we waited six years before we married. I was blessed with this marriage and a beautiful soul whose love has no limits.

Another general consideration is compatibility, and this encompasses not only physical compatibility but also emotional and intellectual capability. A good partner should share common interests and values and be able to communicate effectively. It is important to find someone who is supportive and encouraging who can help overcome any challenges. When it comes to physical compatibility there are many factors to consider, for example assistance may be needed with certain activities such as getting dressed or preparing meals. A good partner will be willing to help with these tasks and will also be comfortable with any adaptions needed to be made to accommodate any physical limitations. They should also be able to discuss exploring potential changes to maintain intimacy that may have arisen due to the amputation.

It is important to consider the level of independence desired as some prefer to handle things on their own, as much as possible, while others may require more assistance. Some may just prefer to be single, but outside support should still be sought to ease the transition ahead.

What is important is to find a partner who is willing to respect the level of independence sought and aid with assistance when needed without being overbearing or patronising. It can be a fine balance at times, especially when emotions are taut. A good partner will be curious about the amputees' experiences and willing to learn more about their condition as well as how they can provide the best support.

I have been fortunate to find someone who is willing to learn and grow alongside me as I do with her, which means being open to new experiences and opportunities, and being willing to adapt as needs change over time. Love is a wonderful thing.

As we age, our bodies undergo significant changes and we become more vulnerable to a range of health issues. This can be particularly challenging for amputees, who may have additional concerns related to their amputation. The first and foremost fear is one of declining physical abilities. As we age, we naturally begin to slow down, and we may find ourselves struggling to perform tasks which were once routine. This can be particularly challenging as it may impact the ability to use prosthetics or navigate the world with a mobility aid. It is important for the ageing amputee to think and plan forward by considering any changes which may need to be made to accommodate their evolving physical abilities. For instance my thoughts are now about moving from a house to a bungalow to help us both later in life. There is no rush, but forward planning is a good thing.

Another common fear is the potential for secondary health conditions. Amputees are at a higher risk for certain health issues such as cardiovascular disease, diabetes, and osteoporosis. As we age, our risk for these conditions also increases which adds an additional layer of concern. It is important to prioritise health and to work closely with the healthcare team or doctor to manage any underlying health issues.

Mental health is also important to consider because the fear of isolation and loneliness may become more pronounced as we age particularly for those who may be limited in their mobility. They may also experience anxiety or depression related to their reputation as they confront the challenges of ageing. It is important for ageing amputees to stay connected with their social support networks and to prioritise their mental health by seeking out therapy or counselling if needed.

Financial concerns can also be a source of anxiety. As we age our health care needs may become more extensive and the cost of medical care can be significant. It is important to plan for potential healthcare costs and to explore options such as long term care, insurance, or assistance programmes.

Those who are pre, or recently post-amputation who earned their living from motor skills which have been lost with the amputation are vulnerable to adverse reactions. Motor skills are those which involve specific movements of the body's muscles to perform a certain task. The five basic motor skills are sitting, standing, walking, running, and jumping. Those whose main line of work is not particularly dependent on the function of the lost limb may experience less emotional difficulty. For instance, my first job after losing my leg was as a draughtsperson where I sat in front of a drawing board all day. Losing my leg made no difference in performing this work.

In reflecting on the work front, if someone loses a limb in later life, even after retirement, this will mean declining mobility, which is linked to a poorer quality of life. This underlines the importance of ongoing care and rehabilitation. We also need to understand the psychological consequences of war trauma in veterans, which can be very long lasting. Those with a physical disability may experience even greater distress as their injuries become more disabling through ageing.

It is a fact of life elderly people with a lower limb amputation impose a heavy burden on health resources, requiring extensive rehabilitation and long term care. Mobility is key to regaining independence however, the impact of multiple illnesses in this group can make regaining mobility a particularly challenging task.

If I look back on my life, having been an amputee for four times more than when I was able-bodied, it does draw upon many experiences I would otherwise not have had. As life is made up of experiences, I embrace those and look back on how I have evolved. I will of course never know what experiences I would have had if I had not lost my leg. The overwhelming thought is I cannot change what has happened, so it is not worth going down that rabbit hole for a fruitless journey of 'what-ifs'. I cannot deny I occasionally go there, but never for very long because I believe it is a downward spiral visiting that place with no clear cut answers.

I do believe with age I have embraced my disability and accepted it knowing I can never replace what was physically lost. Remember life is not a problem to be solved, but a reality to be experienced. I wish you all well on life's journey because no one can go back and start a new beginning, but anyone can start today and make a new positive ending.

Jim - *Time to reflect. This has been an interesting and challenging exercise which has turned out to be different than what I thought it would be. It has required me to give much more thought to recollecting everything which has happened to me in the last five plus years since my amputation. During this time, I would have random thoughts on various amputee related subjects and try to define how I felt about it trying to solidify my position on a particular subject. Many times I would end up with more questions than answers, but I continued to work on it.*

During the four or five months working on this project, I have been able to solidify and organize my thoughts by writing them down. It is interesting how committing thoughts to paper makes everything become more focused and clearer and not just be randomly bouncing around between your ears, or like Agatha Christie's Hercule Poirot calls them, 'The little grey cells.'

I have concluded there has been very little change in my approach to life and my basic nature from pre to post-amputation. My beliefs, values, attitudes, character traits, sense of humour, creative and logical thinking abilities, positive outlook, intellectual characteristics and all those little grey cells are still intact. However, in my contact with hundreds of other amputees via various social media platforms and personal contact as a peer support volunteer, I have learned many other amputees have varying degrees of difficulty or are unable to bridge that gap and the results are debilitating. For some it is like jumping over a mud puddle whereas for others it is like jumping over the Grand Canyon.

I truly believe the most critical factor which influences a person's ability to bridge the gap between pre and post-amputation is pain. Unrelenting pain can be the most powerful will-breaker known to man. If I had the kind of pain many of you have described, I can guarantee my story would be as different as night and day. I cannot even begin to tell you how thankful I am that I do not suffer any pain related to my amputation.

This year on the twenty third of November is my eighty third birthday. That just happens to be 'Thanksgiving Day' here in the United States of America. Every waking hour of that day I will be giving thanks for my good fortune and praying for those of you who are suffering with amputation related pain and all the other conditions pain causes.

Here is the flip side of the coin. My physical story is one hundred and eighty degrees different than my mental story. I have reconciled myself to the reality where I will not be able to walk any significant distance, even with a walker or rollator. If you recall my early comments, (see chapter 3), in 2017-18, I was in and out of hospitals and rehab centres for a year prior to amputation. During that year, my physical condition deteriorated, and I never regained it. This created all kinds of problems post-amputation. I suffered five years with poor fitting sockets, so I never did get proper physical therapy training. Currently, aside from sleeping, I spend about ninety-five percent of my time in a wheelchair. I use a prosthetic leg to get in and out of my hand control car and other transfer needs. I enjoy coming up with creative ideas to be able to function as normal as possible but still trying to figure out how to get the cereals from the top shelf of the cabinet.

And finally, thank you John Paffett, for letting me ride along on your endeavour to help us ageing amputees deal with the journey until it is time to pay the toll and cross over the bridge. I do not know what forces brought us two together over 5095 miles or 8199 kilometres and eight time zones, but it has been interesting and fun. Finished. HIP – HIP – HOORAY!

James (Jim) D. Clark

Made in the USA
Las Vegas, NV
14 May 2024